The labour movement in Lebanon

Manchester University Press

Identities and Geopolitics in the Middle East

Series editors: Simon Mabon, Edward Wastnidge and May Darwich

After the Arab Uprisings and the ensuing fragmentation of regime-society relations across the Middle East, identities and geopolitics have become increasingly contested, with serious implications for the ordering of political life at domestic, regional and international levels, best seen in conflicts in Syria and Yemen. The Middle East is the most militarised region in the world where geopolitical factors remain predominant factors in shaping political dynamics. Another common feature of the regional landscape is the continued degeneration of communal relations as societal actors retreat into sub-state identities, whilst difference becomes increasingly violent, spilling out beyond state borders. The power of religion – and trans-state nature of religious views and linkages – thus provides the means for regional actors (such as Saudi Arabia and Iran) to exert influence over a number of groups across the region and beyond. This series provides space for the engagement with these ideas and the broader political, legal and theological factors to create space for an intellectual re-imagining of socio-political life in the Middle East.

Originating from the SEPAD project (www.sepad.org.uk), this series facilitates the re-imagining of political ideas, identities and organisation across the Middle East, moving beyond the exclusionary and binary forms of identity to reveal the contingent factors that shape and order life across the region.

Previously published titles

Houses built on sand: Violence, sectarianism and revolution in the Middle East
Simon Mabon

The Gulf States and the Horn of Africa: Interests, influences and instability
Robert Mason and Simon Mabon (eds)

Transitional justice in process: Plans and politics in Tunisia
Mariam Salehi

Surviving repression: The Egyptian Muslim Brotherhood after the 2013 *coup*
Lucia Ardovini

The labour movement in Lebanon

Power on hold

Lea Bou Khater

MANCHESTER UNIVERSITY PRESS

Published by Manchester University Press
Oxford Road, Manchester M13 9PL

www.manchesteruniversitypress.co.uk

British Library Cataloguing-in-Publication Data
A catalogue record for this book is available from the British Library

ISBN 978 1 5261 5943 4 hardback

First published 2022

Typeset
by Cheshire Typesetting Ltd, Cuddington, Cheshire

To the firefighters who perished in the Beirut explosion and to everything they represent

Contents

Tables

Acknowledgements

First and foremost, my sincere gratitude goes to Gilbert Achcar, Professor of Development Studies and International Relations at the School of Oriental and African Studies, for his unwavering academic support.

I am grateful to Hannes Baumann, senior lecturer at the University of Liverpool, who insisted on the importance of me undertaking this work. Dr Baumann, together with John Chalcraft, Professor of Middle East History and Politics at London School of Economics and Political Science, kindly read the book proposal and manuscript and provided incredibly valuable feedback. I particularly appreciate the encouragement of Marwan Kraidy, Dean of Northwestern University in Qatar, who without knowing it, gave me the ultimate drive to finally submit my proposal. I am thankful to the two unnamed reviewers assigned by Manchester University Press for their input and for believing in this project. I am indebted to Therese Bjorn Mason, who read successive drafts of the manuscript and ensured that it was in excellent shape for publication thanks to her superb copyediting skills and incredible attention to detail. I am fortunate to have the support of and reality checks from my friends Rania Nader and Corine Rahi, who helped in more ways than they can imagine. I am immensely grateful to my family. My ultimate gratitude goes to Elie and Nadira, whom I am so proud to call my parents, and who selflessly provided all the love and support I needed.

Abbreviations

CAS	Central Administration of Statistics
CR	Council of Representatives
FPM	Free Patriotic Movement
FTUWE	Federation of Trade Unions of Workers and Employees
GCWL	General Confederation of Workers in Lebanon
ILO	International Labour Organization
LBP	Lebanese pound
LCP	Lebanese Communist Party
MEHE	Ministry of Education and Higher Education
NSSF	National Social Security Fund
PIC	Price Index Committee
PSP	Progressive Socialist Party
SSNP	Syrian Social Nationalist Party
UCC	Union Coordination Committee

Introduction: Where are the workers?

Shortly after 6pm on 4 August 2020, a colossal explosion at the Port of Beirut tore through the city, claiming more than two hundred lives and wounding around six thousand. The supersonic blast waves eviscerated much of the port, pulverising Lebanon's grain reserves, and severely damaging commercial and dense residential areas within a five-kilometre radius, leaving hundreds of thousands displaced. It is staggering to walk around the scene of the blast. Physical damages were estimated at US$4.6 billion and economic losses at US$3.5 billion, given the economic activity in the area and that the port is the main point of entry for Lebanon's small open economy, funnelling two-thirds of the country's total trade.

A fire detonated purportedly 2,750 tonnes of ammonium nitrate stored at the port's Hangar 12. Experts estimated the explosion was equivalent to 10 per cent of the intensity of the Hiroshima bomb and described it as one of the largest non-nuclear blasts in history. The explosion could have been averted by taking simple precautions – ammonium nitrate is often used as an agricultural fertiliser and is a relatively safe substance when stored properly. It should have been disposed of or resold, or the storage warehouses at least equipped with a fire-extinguishing system. Irrespective of whether the explosion was an accident or act of sabotage, storing such a massive amount of dangerous incendiary material in the heart of the capital[1] has become a poignant manifestation of a dysfunctional political system – a system marred by high levels of corruption, incompetence and neglect and which solely serves the interests of a post-war oligarchy of businessmen and financiers, who divide between them the rents and spoils of a rolled-back state and uncompetitive markets.

Prior to the Beirut explosion, this dysfunctional system and the resulting social and economic grievances had already culminated in social unrest, referred to as the October Revolution. On 14 October 2019, Lebanon witnessed a national catastrophe when thousands of square metres of forest were scorched by hundreds of fires, the worst in decades, again confirming the failure of the state to protect its citizens. Three firefighting helicopters donated to the state had been left to fall into disrepair as successive governments failed to fund their maintenance. Residents and local civil-defence teams were left to fight the fires and organise shelter, food, water and medical attention and supplies. A few days later, on 17 October 2019, thousands of Lebanese citizens took to the streets after the cabinet approved a new tax of US$0.20 per day on internet-based calls over services like WhatsApp. Mobile phone users in Lebanon pay some of the highest tariffs in the world, and yet adding a tax to WhatsApp usage was regarded by the Government as the first step in a set of higher taxes and budget cuts. While the largest protests took place in Beirut, where thousands gathered in Riyad al-Solh and Martyrs' Square, road blocks rapidly spread to other regions, where protesters gathered in peripheral cities for the first time – from Tripoli in the north to Saida and Tyre in the south, and Baalbek in the west. In unprecedented events, people poured into the streets, shouting in anger and chanting profane slogans targeting the *entire* ruling class.

This book seeks to explain how workers' participation in the social turmoil preceding the outbreak of unruly protests in October 2019 and the impact of the demise of trade union power on the unfolding of the October Revolution are far more important than most observers have acknowledged. The absence of a labour movement has determined the amount of collective action in the post-war period and has influenced the subsequent recent attempts to mobilise. The demise of the labour movement not only threatens working conditions but also affects, even if indirectly, the quality, scope and action of civil society and political life in general. The weakening of the workers, who are the largest and most significant civil actors, hampers the potential and strength of social movements in their struggle for change. Therefore, workers and their trade unions are the principal subjects of this book. I explain the trajectory of the workers' movement in Lebanon by answering two questions. What are the obstacles that shaped state–labour relations and the trajectory and scope of the labour movement? And what is the impact of the state's co-optation of the labour movement on the unfolding of the political and economic system in the post-war period, and the 'contentious politics'[2] targeting these systems today?

The uprising was, of course, not caused merely by the new tax; instead, it was the igniting spark. Lebanese had been pushed to breaking point by a long-standing laissez-faire economic model characterised by capture of the elite and an unfettered capitalist system relying on the financial sector, which exacerbated social grievances and the inability of the state to care for those left behind. Lebanese were already reeling from long-standing social and economic vulnerabilities, such as poor-quality services – including a dysfunctional electricity sector and water supply shortages – plus a chronic lack of job opportunities and continuous migration. The eruption of the conflict in Syria in 2011 and the inflow of refugees had also exposed Lebanon's economic vulnerabilities. In 2014, 10 per cent of the Lebanese adult population held 45 per cent of the wealth, and by 2018, 1 per cent of depositors held 52 per cent of deposits.[3] By contrast, 44 per cent of the population lacked any social protection. With restricted and inadequate social protection, the Lebanese diaspora has long been providing a social security net for their families. In 2018, the World Bank estimated remittances to Lebanon at US$7.2 billion, but this safety net has social consequences. Alejandro Portes argues that remittances tend to have an alleviating effect on the recipient country, helping to consolidate the ruling elite despite increasingly deteriorating political and economic conditions. The consequence is taming or at least delaying the struggle for change. As soon as remittances drop, poverty previously cushioned by the transfers from migrants hits hard.[4] Remittances to Lebanon decreased from 24.7 per cent of GDP in 2008 to 13.9 per cent in 2019.[5] In a survey conducted during the first ten days of the October Revolution, more than 87 per cent of respondents said that poor economic conditions were behind their participation in the protests. Corruption was the second most cited response (61 per cent), followed by the tax system (59 per cent).[6] The outbreak of popular protests unfolded against the backdrop of an economic meltdown. The trigger of the currency crisis was the closure of banks for fourteen days following the onset of the protests. Although no banking system can sustain an uncontrolled run on the banks, the situation in Lebanese banks was especially dire because of the sustained pressure on their foreign reserves caused by the negative balance of payments since 2011. Lebanon experienced a drop in foreign currency inflows, including Foreign Direct Investments (FDI) and remittances and a fall in exports, mainly due to the closure of trading routes through Syria. In March 2020, the state defaulted on a US$1.2 billion Eurobond sovereign debt for the first time. In protest against calamitous economic conditions exacerbated by the impact of the COVID-19 pandemic, people took to the streets again in June of the same year, as the Lebanese pound plummeted to a record low, losing 80 per cent of its value. The devaluation caused prices of basic staples to soar, reaching a record high year-on-year inflation of 123 per cent as well as a shortage of essential medical supplies.[7] Against this backdrop, the port explosion wrecked a population already grappling with the convergence of systemic failures and a devastating economic meltdown. A few days after the blast, people gathered in Beirut to protest against government corruption and criminal neglect and to express their anger over the explosion. Security forces stand accused of having used excessive violence, including tear gas, live ammunition, metal pellets and rubber bullets.

On 5 August, the day after the explosion, the Government declared Beirut to be under a two-week state of emergency. This granted the army exceptional powers, including trying civilians in military courts for crimes said to breach security; prohibiting gatherings; setting curfews; censoring the media; imposing house arrest; and entering homes at any given time. While the technocratic cabinet resigned in the aftermath of the explosion, the political system remained unchanged as the ruling elite clung to the reins of power more than ever. The caretaker Government extended the state of emergency for an additional month.[8]

Despite the absence of substantial change, a chief achievement of the October Revolution was the paradigm shift it generated. After decades of simply following sectarian leaders, citizens began to become empowered, opposing the political system and voicing their demands. It seemed that there would be no return to the status quo. With the unfolding of the October Revolution in 2019, Lebanon joined the Arab uprisings in their call for representative governments and social equity. 'Despite important differences and specificities of the various uprisings, a unifying thread runs through all of them: a call for dignity, empowerment, political citizenship, social justice, and taking back the state from presidents-for-life, as well as from their families and crony capitalists who hijacked it.'[9]

The Lebanese uprising has brought to the fore the conspicuous absence of Lebanon's labour movement in political dissent. The General Confederation of Workers in Lebanon (GCWL) did not call for any strikes or demonstrations in support of the popular protests and waited nineteen days after the start of the uprising to issue a brief statement demanding the formation of a new cabinet.[10] The striking silence of Lebanon's labour movement is critical at this juncture – we know that labour mobilisation played a crucial role in the 2011 revolutions in Egypt and Tunisia and that it has been a key feature of Sudan's 2018–19 uprising since. 'Labor strikes and work stoppages raged in manufacturing, mining, post, port, subway, commercial, and other enterprises. The Egyptian government reported 335 labor protests, 258 sit-ins, and close to 4,500 individual and group complaints to the Ministry of Manpower during 2011.'[11] Why was the labour movement absent from the Lebanese uprising? What does this reveal about the economic and political systems in Lebanon? What impact does this absence have on the uprising? And how does the uprising affect the labour movement itself?

In previous years, most popular protests in Lebanon had lacked a representative structure. Protests were sometimes led by civil society organisations but impaired by labour associations' lack of involvement. In fact, with the spread of the Arab uprisings, several scholars suggest that the world is witnessing new forms of protest, without organisation or central leadership.[12] The limited capabilities of structureless and leaderless movements in dealing with soaring economic and social grievances were illustrated in cases such as Egypt, Tunisia and Yemen. 'But these astonishing rapid triumphs ... did not leave much opportunity for the oppositions, if they ever intended to build parallel organs of authority capable of taking control of the new states.'[13] This highlights the importance and the need to go back to political and labour organising which can guarantee a sustained and coordinated pressure over a longer time period, while also helping to cement a social movement throughout the country. The co-optation of labour unions that began at the end of the Lebanese Civil War aimed to curtail exactly that.

Implications of the argument

In a world dominated by neoliberalism, there is a renewed curiosity in labour organising and radical forms of action outside the institutional framework. The key role of the labour movement for political and economic change is still relevant today, despite the significant changes that have altered the global socio-economic system. In their collective work, Joel Beinin and Frederic Vairel reiterate the durability of economic reasons that fuel labour organising.

International financial institutions, as well as postmodern radical democratic theory, despite their divergent perspectives, share the view that the mobilisation of workers is an idea whose time has passed and that the working class as an organising principle or class solidarity slogan is no longer fashionable. Nevertheless, the economic reasons for mobilisation that informed the previous constructions of the working class as a political category have not disappeared.[14]

Some of the most salient consequences of neoliberal policies for workers and the labour movement include arbitrary dismissal, mandatory lay-offs, workforce reductions, militant labour struggles and violent state intervention.[15] While changes or structural shifts in the global economy have downsized the scope and activity of unions, scholars posit that although important changes have taken place in politics and at the international and national levels, trade unions remain key actors in the economic and political realm.[16]

In the Arab world, basic questions about contentious politics were brought to the fore by uprisings that broke out in 2011, which cast a new light on the role of collective action, unruly politics and new popular political imagination in shaping political fields, while stepping away from the usual straitjacketed elements of analysis such as elite politics, foreign meddling or security forces.[17] The past fixation with top-down politics was superseded by a new academic interest in bottom-up politics, ordinary people and workers. 'What distinguished the large-scale popular uprisings

in 2011 from past small-scale protests was the active participation by urban
and rural workers and the poor in general. That was a tipping point overlooked by the old regimes and their security apparatus, surprising even the
young revolutionaries who had been agitating to mobilize the public.'[18]
In this context, new energy and attention have been given to the complex
role of labour and social movement in the dynamics of change. Trade-
union politics has seen an unexpected resurgence in the wider Arab world.
Many observers emphasise the role of the labour movement in dissent in
the decade preceding the Arab uprising and its impact on recent popular
protests.

While Lebanon has been the attention of much research, questions about
labour relations have rarely been touched upon by academia. Literature
dealing with trade unions and labour relations in Lebanon in the post-war
period is scant and I have engaged with most of its authors in the writing
of this book. Studies of the Lebanese Civil War and sectarianism make up
most of the research on Lebanon and have the effect of impinging the sectarian logic onto scholarship and largely overlooking other elements that could
explain the history of Lebanon's labour relations.

In Lebanon, it was the labour movement that first mobilised against
post-war reconstruction policies, but the movement was soon co-opted. The
co-optation paved the way for a smooth implementation of a laissez-faire
economic model without any popular opposition or collective bargaining
for social and economic demands. Despite mounting social and economic
grievances, organised labour was in alliance with the post-war 'allotment
state' (*dawlat al-muhasasa*) and its elite. At the end of the civil war, the
political system rested on the 'shared domination and deal-making' between
the president of the republic, president of the parliament and the prime
minister – also referred to as the troika.[19] 'The outcomes of their inces-
sant bargaining followed a logic of partitioning the spoils of public office,
privileges and resources, a phenomenon called *muhasasa* (allotment).'[20] The
unfolding of the October Revolution exposed the indifference of the labour
movement because of its cosy alliance with the state elite and the weakness
of popular protests without the support and backing of organised labour.

In general, different factors shape labour relations, such as the political
system, the institutional framework, economic development, the balance
of power and the socio-cultural context.[21] Therefore, the current situation
of labour relations is a result of earlier struggles under previous socio-
economic conditions. Thus, workers' struggles in the past define the
current and future struggles. The performance and trajectory of the labour
movement can be understood by examining the institutional and legal
framework that regulates the labour movement and its relation with the
state. This book adopts an approach that explains the behaviour of the

labour movement by looking at the institutional framework in which trade unions are created and operate, as well as probing their political affiliations or alliances. The history of labour legislation, the relations between state and labour and between trade unions and political parties in a specific country can explain why trade unions in different settings behave or react differently.[22] This approach highlights the importance of the legal and institutional framework in the study of labour relations and the labour movement. According to Alain Touraine, the labour movement is determined chiefly by the interplay between labour and the state.[23] Finally, the study of the different dimensions of contemporary labour relations and organisation in Lebanon, especially their institutional and legal framework, can highlight the trajectory and performance of the labour movement amid fundamental sectarian boundaries, which have rarely been the subject of research and scholarship. Drawing upon an institutional approach, this book is attentive to the impact of the legal and institutional framework on labour relations. In the institutional perspective, institutions are 'formal or informal procedures, routines, norms and conventions embedded in the organisational structure of the polity or political economy. They can range from the rules of a constitutional order or the standard operating procures of a bureaucracy to the conventions governing trade union behaviour or bank–firm relations.'[24] Institutionalism considers the institutional structure of regimes to have different implications, particularly in terms of the political incorporation of various social structures. An institutionalist approach demonstrates the agreement of rulers across time on the necessity of containing labour power. Decomposing labour power through laws, regulations and organisational structures, which intensified in Lebanon's post-war period, proves the potential threat of labour power to the economic and financial interests of the elite. It also explains why the brutal laissez-faire economic model was able to thrive for decades in Lebanon, leading to an 'explosion of the poor' in 2019 – that may be a breakthrough for the re-composition of labour power.

Ruth Berins Collier and David Collier resort to institutionalism to explain the behaviour of labour movements through the institutional framework in which trade unions are created, as well as their past political affiliations or alliances. In this regard, Collier and Collier's study shows the impact of state incorporation during early industrialisation on the trajectory of labour movements in Latin America. By state incorporation, Collier and Collier refer to the extent of political unity among different elites towards imposing a new political and institutional framework on the labour movement.[25] The study examines the labour movement in eight Latin American countries – Chile, Brazil, Venezuela, Mexico, Uruguay, Colombia, Peru and Argentina – all of which witnessed a shift from the repression of the labour movement to its incorporation. Through this comparative analysis, the authors examine the repercussions of the different strategies of control and mobilisation in terms of political coalitions, party systems and modes of political conflict, through what the Colliers refer to as 'critical juncture', a short period of change where previous conditions allow for choices that set a trajectory of institutional development that is difficult to change. In his examination of the labour movement in Tunisia and Egypt, Beinin explains that the potential and limitations of workers are defined by their organisational capacities and their relationships with political parties and civil society, as well as changes in the local and global economy.

The political economy of the workers' movements in Tunisia and Egypt is similar. But the possibilities and limitations on workers' agency were structured by their organisational capacities, their relationships with the intelligentsia, political parties and non-governmental organisations (NGOs), as well as changes in the local and global political economy. These factors explain why the Tunisian General Labour Union (Union Générale Tunisienne du Travail, UGTT) decisively influenced Tunisia's post–Ben Ali trajectory towards procedural democracy. In contrast, the Egyptian Trade Union Federation (ETUF) remained loyal to Mubarak until the end, and beyond. Newly established independent unions and federations did not have the organisational capacity or political experience to influence the post-Mubarak political agenda or prevent the installation of a praetorian autocracy more vicious than the Mubarak regime.[26]

According to Eva Bellin, the level of institutionalisation defines and determines the robustness of the coercive apparatus in repressing reform initiatives. More precisely, a coercive apparatus endowed with a limited level of institutionalisation is characterised by patrimonialism, cronyism, a blurred distinction between public and private – leading to corruption and abuse of power – and discipline 'that is maintained through the exploitation of primordial cleavages, often relying on balanced rivalry between different ethnic/sectarian groups'.[27] In these conditions, any political reform is perceived as a prospect of ruin for the elite of the coercive apparatus, which also has the advantage of taming the opposition. In turn, patrimonial institutions are less receptive to political change and democratic initiatives. Conversely, a high level of institutionalisation would show more tolerance for reforms.[28]

Bellin's analysis underlines the significance of revising structural factors and the character of state institutions for researching democratic transition and also for the prospects of any democratic initiatives that stem from the labour movement. As previously mentioned, this research examines the effect of institutions – designed by a long-lasting sectarian ruling elite – on the capacity of the sectarian elite to tame any reform initiatives, including those that stem from the mobilisation of the labour movement. Thus, this research focuses on the structural and institutional conditions which formed and surrounded the labour movement in Lebanon.

Drawing upon this framework, this research speaks to three different concerns. Most broadly, it seeks to engage the debate on processes of sectarianisation. Rather than focusing on sectarianism, this work looks to understand the process and mechanisms of sectarianisation. As Rima Majed observes, 'it seems crucial to start by de-sectarianising research methods in order to be able to observe and detect the non-sectarian factors, mechanisms, and dynamics that shape the process of "sectarianisation" and that give the illusion of the predominance of a static and enduring "sectarianism"'.[29] I posit that the institutionalisation of sectarianism is used by the ruling elite to protect its economic and financial interests in an open economy. It is not sectarian identity per se that weakens the labour movement. This allows for a debunking of the traditional strict perspective of sectarianism and identity politics. Therefore, the innovative theoretical approach of this book is to examine and consider labour relations in Lebanon, giving specific attention to the role of state incorporation in the preservation of the sectarian liberal system. Hiding beneath the sectarian veil and under the guise of preserving confessional balances, the post-war ruling elite of businessmen and financiers organised state incorporation of the labour movement to guarantee their command of the main economic resources and the hollowed-out state.

The second goal of this research is to contest the predominant view of the trajectory of the labour movement in Lebanon. It challenges the perceived wisdom on the rise of the labour movement in the 1950s and 1960s and its subsequent fall during the post-war period from the 1990s onwards.[30] In other words, what is perceived as a fall after the end of the civil war was merely the intensification of liberal economic policies and escalating political intervention by the state elite, which had already been in place since independence in 1943. I posit that, from its very beginning, the labour movement had never been endowed with resilient pillars for growth and development.

The third goal is to reflect on the lessons of this research for Arab and other countries in general and specifically for those governed by sectarian power-sharing, such as Iraq. Similar to other Arab countries, the formation of the labour movement in Lebanon is influenced by colonial capitalism and the impact of the nationalist struggle for liberation as identified by several authors, including Joel Beinin, Zachary Lockman and Ellis Goldberg. In Lebanon, the birth of the labour movement was significantly shaped by the French mandate and the struggle for independence. However, the importance of examining organised labour in Lebanon stems from the distinctiveness of the Lebanese context with respect to sectarian power-sharing and a pervasive liberal economic system that did not include state-sponsored development and industrialisation. While neighbouring countries such as Egypt, Syria and Tunisia were gradually moving towards a 'socialist experiment' in the 1950s and 1960s – adopting planned economies, import-substitution industrialisation or a so-called 'peripheral Keynesianism' – nationalisation schemes funnelled capital into Lebanon and reified the small open economy, which soon adopted a banking secrecy law in 1956, attracting the channelling of funds to the country. Lebanon had faithfully maintained an open-market economy and rolled-back state, which largely defined working-class formation and labour power. 'Locally, Lebanon's laissez-faire policy of free trade, deregulation of currency exchange, unrestricted capital flow, and total absence of any banking regulation were hailed as the engines of this growth.'[31] This sheds light on the continuous attempts by the state elite to decompose labour power in Lebanon ever since independence in 1943, coupled with poor and fragmented social protection policies. When the failure of developmentalism was declared following the 1970s oil crisis and global recession, a new economic strategy was promoted in the global south, based on market-driven and export-led growth. Lebanon witnessed the eruption of the civil war and chose a different path to the Arab region, which also shaped state–labour relations.

A word on methodology

The argument presented here grows out of extensive fieldwork in Lebanon, beginning with a three-year period between 2013 and 2016, and supplemented by follow-up fieldwork in 2019–20. The research design relies on two distinct types of data collection. First, I consulted archival and secondary sources. I accessed previously untapped archives of the GCWL and the Ministry of Labour from the 1990s on, as well as articles, opinion pieces and editorials in the mainstream media from 1990 to 2017, which allowed for a historically grounded account of the trajectory of the GCWL. I consulted secondary-source literature, although limited, in Arabic, English and French. Documents include pre-existing labour studies in Lebanon such as historical timelines, socio-economic reports, official labour force data published by the Central Administration of Statistics (CAS) and other reliable sources on labour relations. Unlike English and French, scholarly publications in the Arabic language are almost non-existent. Most of the relevant scholarship in Arabic is published by unionists aiming to document their personal experience or the history of the labour movement in Lebanon, which provides essential contextualisation. On that score, I engaged with the early work of the pioneer unionist Fu'ad Shimali, as well as renowned unionists such as Elias Boueiri and Elias Haber.

The data collection process had, at times, significant limitations. First, the Ministry of Labour does not consolidate nor publish the data on the number of trade unions, federations and their membership size. The access to trade union data at the Ministry of Labour was granted for only one week, which was an extremely short period of time, taking into account the lack of classification and digitisation of the data. The Ministry of Labour is the source of data pertaining to trade unions and their members. Prior to every election, every trade union is required to submit a list of its members to the Ministry of Labour. This is a legal requirement of the ministry for its endorsement of the results of the elections. In turn, the Ministry of Labour is supposed to have the updated details of active trade unions. However, many problems arose. The ministry's data pertaining to federations and trade unions are not computerised. In order to acquire the number of members per trade union, the latest electoral lists pertaining to the latest election have to be located and the number of members calculated.[32] The data are available for 59 out of 60 federations. The remaining data are lost. Second, the most recent number of trade union members can only be found for the year of the last board election. Trade unions can have irregular elections and therefore the number of members listed in the electoral lists can go back many years. Third, obtaining access to the trade union data is a tedious job. An authorisation is required from the general director for every user, an authorisation that is usually difficult to obtain and often requires personal connections. Access to the GCWL archives was not granted. Instead, I relied on the personal collection of a previous GCWL staff member.

Second, I conducted interviews with pivotal actors in trade union politics, including former ministers of labour, trade unionists, GCWL staff and representatives of international organisations involved in labour politics. The interviews were semi-structured and open-ended. Interviewees were selected on a convenience basis and were chosen for the knowledge of a subject, such as former and current ministers of labour and general directors, former and current unionists, former and current business association representatives, and so on. Secondly, the selection of activists and workers in specific economic sectors followed the snowballing technique while ensuring that this was not restricted to one segment of the targeted population. The research aimed at targeting key informants and stakeholders who had taken part in the labour movement before, during and after the civil war in order to be able to provide relevant information. Some participants met with me several times, at length, while other stakeholders refused to participate, such as the former GCWL President Elias abu Rizq, while others delayed the agreed date and time of the meeting and were unable to meet, such as the current GCWL president Bishara al-Asmar.

Plan of the book

The book begins with an exploration of the logic that steered the state incorporation of the labour movement in Lebanon. The first chapter documents state–labour relations throughout key periods between independence in 1943 and the end of the civil war in 1990. This chapter starts with the birth of the workers' movement and the first associations under the Ottoman Empire and reviews the restrictions under the French mandate. It depicts the workers' movement after independence in 1943, including the struggle for the Labour Code, the emergence of union federations and the establishment of the GCWL in Lebanon, as well as its main demands before the outbreak of the war in 1975. The chapter encompasses the mobilisation and protests of the labour movement during the civil war. The second chapter addresses the demands and struggle of the labour movement during the post-war reconstruction period. The chapter aims at examining the tools and strategies to which the state elite resorted during critical periods in order to capture the labour movement. The third chapter tackles the developments since 2011, when a revival of organised labour took place among public-sector workers. As far as possible, the chapter dissects the contextual factors and the structural elements that may explain the mobilisation of public-sector employees, as well as the impact and outcomes of the 2015 mobilisation. Finally, the last chapter explores the implications of a muted labour movement for the present and future struggle for change.

Notes

1 Lebanese officials impounded the cargo ship *MV Rhosus* for breach of standards set by the International Maritime Organization (IMO) and defaulting on charges, including port fees. Port authorities had subsequently moved the cargo of ammonium nitrate from the vessel to a port warehouse. L. Khalili, 'Behind the Beirut explosion lies the lawless world of international shipping', *Guardian* (8 August 2020).

2 Coined by Charles Tilly in works he began in the 1970s, the concept focuses on social movements and extends to include strikes, civil wars, revolutions and insurgencies. In their book, Charles Tilly and Sidney Tarrow define the concept as follows: 'Contentious politics involves interactions in which actors make

claims bearing on other actors' interests, leading to coordinated efforts on behalf of shared interests or programs, in which governments are involved as targets, initiators of claims, or third parties. Contentious politics thus brings together three familiar features of social life: contention, collective action, and politics.' C. Tilly and S. Tarrow, *Contentious Politics* (New York: Oxford University Press, 2015), p. 7.

3 Data from a leaked 2020 document by the Banking Control Commission of Lebanon.

4 A. Portes, 'Migration and development: reconciling opposite views', *Ethnic and Racial Studies*, 32:1 (2009), 5–22.

5 Personal remittances comprise all current transfers in cash or in kind made or received by resident households to or from non-resident households. Personal remittances thus include all current transfers between resident and non-resident individuals. World Bank, Databank, data.worldbank.org (accessed 13 November 2020).

6 L. Bou Khater and R. Majed, 'Lebanon's 2019 October Revolution: Who mobilized and why?', Asfari Institute for Civil Society and Citizenship, Working Papers (Beirut: Asfari Institute, 2020).

7 Consultation and Research Institute, 'Consumer Price Index Monthly Report – July 2020' (Beirut: Consultation and Research Institute, 2020).

8 The state of emergency decree issued on 20 August became null as Parliament did not ratify it within eight days of its publication in the official journal.

9 F. Gerges, *The New Middle East: Protests and Revolution in the Arab World* (Cambridge: Cambridge University Press, 2014), p. 4.

10 GCWL, Statement of the executive bureau dated 5 November 2019, www.cgtl-lb.org/NewsDetails.aspx?NewsID=13370 (accessed 13 November 2020).

11 A. Bayat, *Life as Politics: How Ordinary People Change the Middle East* (Stanford, CA: Stanford University Press, 2013), p. 271.

12 *Ibid.*, p. 268.

13 *Ibid.*, p. 273.

14 J. Beinin and F. Vairel (eds), *Social Movements, Mobilisation, and Contestation in the Middle East and North Africa* (Stanford, CA: Stanford University Press, 2013), p. 21.

15 A. Bieler, I. Lindberg and D. Pillay, *Labour and the Challenges of Globalization: What Prospects for Transnational Solidarity?* (London: Pluto Press, 2008), pp. 23–44.

16 C. Frege and J. Kelly (eds), *Varieties of Unionism: Strategies for Union Revitalization in a Globalizing Economy* (Oxford: Oxford University Press, 2004), p. 181.

17 J. Chalcraft, *Popular Politics in the Making of the Modern Middle East* (Cambridge: Cambridge University Press, 2016), p. 6.

18 Gerges, *The New Middle East*, p. 6.

19 R. Leenders, *Spoils of Truce: Corruption and State-Building in Postwar Lebanon* (Ithaca, NY: Cornell University Press, 2012), p. 140.

20 *Ibid.*

21 G. Ioannou, 'Labour Relations in Cyprus: Employment, Trade Unionism and Class Composition' (PhD dissertation, University of Warwick, 2011), p. 17.

22 G. Seidman, *Manufacturing Militance: Workers' Movements in Brazil and South Africa, 1970–1985* (Berkeley: University of California Press, 1994), p. 20.

23 A. Touraine, M. Wieviorka and F. Dubet, *Le Mouvement Ouvrier* (Paris: Fayard, 1984), p. 10.

24 P. Hall and R. Taylor, 'Political science and the three new institutionalisms', *Political Studies*, 44:5 (2016), 938.

25 R. Collier and D. Collier, *Shaping the Political Arena: Critical Junctures, the Labor Movement, and Regime Dynamics in Latin America* (Princeton, NJ: Princeton University Press, 1991), p. 20.

26 J. Beinin, *Workers and Thieves: Labor Movements and Popular Uprisings in Tunisia and Egypt* (Stanford, CA: Stanford University Press, 2015), pp. 7–8.

27 E. Bellin, 'Coercive Institutions and Coercive Leaders' in M. Posusney and M. Angrist (eds), *Authoritarianism in the Middle East: Regimes and Resistance* (Boulder, CO: Lynne Rienner, 2005), p. 28.

28 *Ibid.*, pp. 28–34.

29 R. Majed, 'The Theoretical and Methodological Traps in Studying Sectarianism in the Middle East: Neo-Primordialism and "Cliched Constructivism"' in S. Larbi, *Routledge Handbook of Middle East Politics: Interdisciplinary Inscriptions* (London: Routledge, 2020), p. 547.

30 F. Traboulsi, *A History of Modern Lebanon* (London: Pluto Press, 2007); S. Baroudi, 'Economic Conflict in Postwar Lebanon: State–Labor Relations between 1992 and 1997', *Middle East Journal*, 52:4 (1998), 531–50; B. Salloukh, 'Sectarianism and struggles for socio-economic rights' in B. Salloukh et al., *The Politics of Sectarianism in Postwar Lebanon* (London: Pluto Press, 2015).

31 H. Safieddine, *Banking on the State: The Financial Foundations of Lebanon* (Stanford, CA: Stanford University Press, 2019), p. 83.

32 Data consist of archived folders that contain information classified by the Federation of trade unions. Papers inside the folders are randomly archived in no chronological or alphabetical order, and folders are randomly stored without a specific referencing system, which renders the usage of these data a complicated and lengthy process.

1

Shackles for the road

At the beginning of the twentieth century, the first signs of collective action appeared among print workers. During this period, the number of print shops grew, and in 1911 the Association of Printing Press Workers was created. It soon united with the Association of Workers of the American Printing Press, established in the following year.[1] The Association of Railway Workers, which played an important role in the history of the labour movement, was also established during this period. These early workers' associations operated under several laws issued by the Ottoman Empire between 1909 and 1912 governing associations and strike action.[2] The term 'trade union' first appeared in Lebanon in 1919 and therefore these early legal texts refer to workers' organisations as associations.[3] Following the First World War, Lebanon was in a critical economic situation and the population had suffered long years of hunger. In reaction to difficult living conditions, the Association of Railway Workers went on strike in 1920 demanding a wage increase. The strike was suspended as soon as workers were promised a pay rise, but the railway company did not keep its promise and the strike resumed in 1921. This time workers were poorly organised and the strike was only partially respected. Besides, the railway company was determined to curb workers' protests: several unionists were laid off and the company tightened its grip on workers.[4] At the same time, workers in tobacco factories in Bikfaya, a town in the Metn District of Mount Lebanon, started to organise under the leadership of Fu'ad Shimali, who was one of the main founders of the People's Party established in 1924.[5] The People's Party would become the Lebanese Communist Party (LCP) in 1925. At the end of the First World War and following the Sykes–Picot Agreement of 1916, a French mandate was established over Lebanon and Syria. On 31 August 1920, the State of Greater Lebanon was declared under the French mandate. In 1922, the League of Nations approved the mandate, which took effect the following year. Under the French mandate, the labour movement would thrive due to the increasing number of print shops in Beirut, the exposure of the print workers to the experience of other countries, the growth of Beirut following the decline of the silk industry and, not least, the impact of the Bolshevik revolution.

During this period, the trajectory and discourse of the labour movement were influenced by the French experience but were also moulded amid the institutionalisation of sectarianism – the process and mechanisms of sectarianisation through legal texts and institutions. Under the French mandate, the institutionalisation of sectarianism expanded the practice of sectarian distribution of deputies' seats perpetuated during Ottoman rule.

Institutionalised sectarianism

The sectarian violence in Lebanon, from nineteenth-century upheavals in Mount Lebanon – notably the strife of 1860 – to the outbreak of the civil war in the twentieth century, gives the impression that the Lebanese problem is mainly tribal – that sectarianism in itself prevents modernisation, and that Lebanon is an example of a failed nationalism taking into account omnipresent static sectarian identities.[6]

Nevertheless, sectarian identity is a modern and recent construct. In his book *The Culture of Sectarianism*, Ussama Makdisi reconstructs the history of sectarian identity in Ottoman Mount Lebanon, where the violent events of 1860 took place. Makdisi attempts to historicise the nationalist approach to sectarianism by explaining that the religious violence between 1840 and 1860 was not the failure of nationalism, 'but an expression of a new form of local politics and knowledge that arose in a climate of transition and reform in the mid-nineteenth-century Ottoman Empire and that laid the foundations for a (later) discourse of nationalist secularism'.[7]

According to Makdisi, sectarianism was first a practice that stemmed from nineteenth-century Ottoman reform. The practice emerged when the regime of Mount Lebanon, dominated by an elite defined by a secular hierarchy rather than its sectarian affiliation, was discredited by the Ottoman reforms. More specifically, this practice appeared when Maronite and Druze elites, Europeans and Ottomans attempted to delineate the relationship of Maronites and Druze with the modernising Ottoman state. The fall of the old Mount Lebanon regime led to a new form of representation and politics based on religious equality. 'This transformation privileged the sectarian community rather than the elite status, as the basis for any projects of modernisation, citizenship, and civilisation.'[8] Secondly, sectarianism developed into a discourse encompassing the set assumptions and writings that described the new form of politics in the narrative of Ottoman, European and Lebanese modernisation.

Despite theoretical differences, Mahdi Amil, a Marxist intellectual and political activist, reached similar conclusions on sectarianism to those of Makdisi. In his works, Amil examines sectarianism from a materialist perspective. He posits that the Lebanese sectarian system can only be understood by studying the impact of the colonial structure on the different social classes and the role sectarianism played within the colonial relations of production.[9] According to Amil, sectarianism did not have a history distinct from the history of the colonial formation.[10] He considers that the emerging colonial bourgeoisie did not challenge the previous elite, but instead adapted to the religious ideology of this elite.[11]

Following the rebellion of commoners against their feudal lords in Mount Lebanon in 1840, the Ottoman Empire divided Mount Lebanon into two districts (*Qa'imaqamiyya*), using sectarian demarcation lines separating the Druze and Maronites. In 1845, a new *Règlement* introduced the creation of administrative councils based on sectarian identities, therefore reinforcing sectarian divisions. The unstable system of *Qa'imaqamiyya* witnessed several controversies on both intra-community and inter-community levels, leading to war in 1860.[12] While the *Règlement Organique* indicated a rupture with the past and the adoption of new administrative and economic regulations, Makdisi stresses the fact that the document and the intent behind its promulgation aimed for the continuity of the old regime: 'By the admission of its own crafters, the *Règlement* was meant to be the climax of a period of flux and a reconsecration of the sectarian order set in place in 1845.' In fact, the *Règlement Organique* attempted to create an 'elitist sectarian system'.[13]

According to Makdisi, every article in the *Règlement* showed that this new political order was sectarian. The European and Ottoman drafters of the *Règlement* tried to separate the population to create religiously homogeneous districts, as can be read in the fifth article. Under the *Règlement*, the sect defined 'one's public sphere involvement, ability to be appointed to office, to govern, to collect taxes, to punish, even to live and exist as a loyal subject'. Article 11 explicitly stated that 'all members of the courts and administrative assemblies will be chosen and appointed by the leaders of their sect in agreement with the notables of the sect'.[14]

After the events of 1860, sectarian consciousness was omnipresent in the sense that all aspects of society considered that warfare and massacres marked the beginning of a new age. Since the sectarian violence of the nineteenth century, Mount Lebanon had been haunted by the risk of renewed sectarian hostilities, which created a political culture that aimed to forget the strife of 1860. This culture was based on, and continues to be built around, a myth of communal homogeneity, as well as religious tolerance and harmony. Similarly, Amil clarifies that sectarianism is a form of bourgeois domination. Sectarianism worked as a 'political relation of class dependency that links the masses – or part of them – to the bourgeoisie in a relation of sectarian political representation'.[15] According to Amil, the purpose of sectarianism was to hamper the formation of the masses into a force capable of challenging the domination of the bourgeoisie. Drawing upon his work, I posit that sectarianism reproduced and maintained, and impeded or was used to impede, the formation and progress of the labour movement as a force capable of challenging the elite and the state.

The collapse of the Ottoman Empire in 1918 was followed by a French mandate over Lebanon. During the League of Nations mandate, the French adopted and expanded the practice of sectarian distribution of deputy seats perpetuated during Ottoman rule. The French mandate created the Representative Council in 1922, which in 1927 became the first Chamber of Deputies. It consisted of an advisory council of thirty representatives to be elected by universal suffrage. Lebanon was divided into districts, and each community was allotted a specific number of representatives, with a total of 16 Christians, 13 Muslims and one representative from the remaining minority sects.

In his seminal work on the Lebanese constitution, Edmond Rabbath considers the first constitution of Lebanon, adopted in 1926, to be a product of an extensive and almost abusive interpretation of an international document amid a period of political conjuncture, with no direct association with or relevance to the Lebanese case.[16] In its first article, the 1922 Mandate Charter for Syria and Lebanon commanded the drafting of a *Statut Organique* for Syria and Lebanon. On 10 December 1925, following a request by the governor of Greater Lebanon, Léon Cayla, the Council of Representatives (CR) elected a special commission to draft the *Statut Organique*. Official texts mention no details of the commission's preparatory work. The following May, in 1926, High Commissioner Henri de Jouvenel declared that the constitution, made up of 102 articles, was in force.[17]

While articles 10–15 of the Constitution pertained to sectarian communities, the main article that had the effect of institutionalising sectarianism was article 95, which specified that all communities should be equally represented in public employment and the cabinet. According to Edmond Rabbath, this article became the fundamental justification for a pathological development of political sectarianism during the mandate and increasingly after independence, ultimately entering minds and institutions like a metastatic growth. The twenty-year French mandate over Lebanon did little to hinder the effects of sectarianism. Indeed, the mandate probably perceived the institutionalisation of the sectarian communities as a source of greater power and a foundation for easier rule.[18]

Birth defects

In this context, the first issue of *al-Yaqaza* magazine appeared in June 1929. It aimed to promote the actions of the labour movement and called on workers to 'wake up from their long sleep'. In its second issue, *al-Yaqaza* declared itself to be the 'voice of the working class'. The early issues of the magazine revealed the significant efforts of print workers to stimulate and form a working-class consciousness. The following year, the terms 'capitalist' and 'proletariat' came into increasing use. *Al-Yaqaza* played an important role in strengthening the organisation and unity of workers and paved the way for a stronger movement.[19]

In his 1928 pamphlet on trade unions, Fu'ad Shimali explained that 'a trade union is a significant economic, social, and political power. Political parties take from trade unions the strength in their political struggle for the proletarian class. It is a weapon for workers against oppressive capitalists. It is a school, where workers learn about their rights and train to fight on all economic, social, and political levels. It is the only support for workers, and political parties cannot succeed in their actions without the support of the organised workers in trade unions.'[20] Shimali linked the struggle of the labour movement in Lebanon to the struggle of the LCP. In 1930, the trade unions of print workers, tobacco workers, upholsterers and hotel chefs and waiters were already under the influence of the LCP. In fact, these unions maintained strong relations with the party until the 1980s.

In the years between 1930 and 1939, living conditions became increasingly difficult. Internal migration from rural areas to urban regions, mainly Beirut, was registered. While agricultural work was no longer productive, the industrial sector was still small and could only absorb a small share of the workforce. Prices were rising while wages remained stagnant. The difficult living conditions were reflected in the actions of the labour movement that aimed at improving the living conditions of wage earners and guaranteeing their freedom of action.[21] The situation intensified in the early 1930s, with strike action from several trade-unionised workers. In 1931, the railway workers went on strike, followed by chauffeurs in 1932 and print workers in 1933. The authorities violently repressed the workers' protests and tried to splinter worker solidarity by manipulating sectarian identities. In 1935, the French authorities insinuated that the print workers' union would be officially authorised on the condition that its president would be a Christian Maronite. To the contrary, all 360 voters – of which the majority were known to be Christian – elected Muslim Mustafa al-'Aris as president.[22] In contrast to a 'primordial' or 'essentialist' obsession with ancient sectarian identities, this incident is seminal to the analysis of the labour movement's trajectory in Lebanon, as it reveals the role of the French authorities, as a state actor, in the birth of the labour movement and state-building more broadly. The incident draws attention to how state actors and elites actively used the 'sectarian card' for reasons of security, geopolitics and power. Following independence in 1943, the ruling elite continued to move deliberately forward with the sectarianisation and capture of organised labour.

With the 1936 victory of the Popular Front in France and the difficult economic situation following the devaluation of the French franc, the workers' struggle in Lebanon intensified. In 1936, workers called a general strike, demanding a 30 per cent wage increase and shorter working hours. In October 1936, workers occupied factories and created a trade union organisational committee to represent all workers in Beirut. Protests continued throughout 1937 and included a chauffeurs' strike in protest against the tax increase on fuel. In the spring of 1937, the print workers' union addressed Parliament with a list of demands, including shorter working hours, an unemployment scheme, injury and disease compensation, annual leave, the right of association and freedom of speech. These demands shed light on the poor working conditions faced by workers and the lack of social safety nets during this period. During 1939, the labour movement experienced a difficult phase marred by repression. Several prominent trade union leaders were arrested. The economic situation deteriorated, resulting in price increases, lack of food and the development of a black market. The living conditions of workers worsened without an outbreak of popular protests except for a few demonstrations in Beirut and Tripoli. According to Younes, the fact that the dire economic conditions triggered no reaction may suggest the influence of international and regional events on the actions and demands of organised labour.

The notion of social class as used by Lebanese trade unionists did not correspond to the Lebanese context. A proletariat, in the Marxist sense, did not exist in Lebanon. Workers were half-way between agricultural and industrial workers and did not constitute a homogeneous group capable of promoting a popular movement. The discourse and path of trade unionists during this period were largely influenced by the French General Confederation of Labour.[23] The concept of social class is ambiguous in the early literature relating to workers in Lebanon. The term 'working class' was used with ambivalence in the discourse of trade unionists. At times, it was employed to refer to blue-collar as opposed to white-collar workers. At other times, the term was used to distinguish between wage earners and other categories of workers. According to Younes, in his work on the history of trade unions in Lebanon, the concept of the working class in Lebanon is borrowed from western literature. In and around the 1930s, trade unionists in Lebanon started using the term 'working class' under the influence of international trade union bodies, as well as the French Communist Party.

Soon, the use of the 'working-class' concept became dominant among different trade unions. This was more a reflection of the ideological and political influence of international trade union bodies and the experience of the working class in industrialised or developed countries.[24] The notion of the 'working class' in the discourse of trade unions to a certain extent overlooked the limited industrial sector and predominant family and sectarian relations.

Trade unionists used the term 'social class' without a precise definition. The use of the term differed between the two main currents of trade unions. Right-wing reformist trade unions condemned class struggle and promoted social agreement and collaboration between wage earners and employers. They supported negotiations and agreements that took into account the mutual interests of employers and employees. In fact, federations comprising right-wing trade unions collaborated with right-leaning political parties that represented the leading economic and political forces in Lebanon at the time.[25] In contrast, the discourse of left-wing trade unions was ambiguous. It promoted reform rather than a change of the structures in place. In the pre-war period, left-wing trade unions used the notion of 'social class' in a general manner.[26] Their discourse was based on ideological concerns rather than on the Lebanese reality. Despite their discourse, these trade unions showed an attachment to the established political regime while focusing on the need for modernisation.

The arrival of Allied troops in Lebanon during the Second World War invigorated the industrial sector, mainly textile production. With sea routes blocked, Lebanon had to provide for the needs of the population and those of foreign troops. In 1942, migration from rural areas began towards the industrial sectors around Beirut. Part of the workforce settled temporarily close to factories while others remained in their place of origin. This proximity to their place of origin and mobility of workers hampered the formation of workers' agglomerations around the workplace, as was the case in Europe, for instance. Industrialisation did not provoke profound geographical changes in Lebanon.

The logic of state–labour relations in independent Lebanon

Before looking at the history and course of the labour movement from Lebanon's independence until the civil war, it is important to pause to better understand the birth and pillars of the Lebanese sectarian-liberal model. Independent Lebanon in 1943 did not change or alter the institutionalised sectarianism that had been further ingrained during the French mandate. In fact, article 95 of the constitution was amended on

9 November 1943 without changing its main purpose – the sectarian distribution of public employment and cabinet seats. While the amendment
strictly removed the reference to the Mandate Charter, article 95 remained
a main pillar of the Lebanese state.[27] Furthermore, the National Pact (*al-
Mithaq al-Waṭani*) of 1943, an unwritten gentlemen's agreement between
the Christian Maronite and Muslim Sunni leaders, stipulated the allocation of the post of president of the republic to a Maronite, and the post of
prime minister to a Sunni. Based on the 1932 census, where Christians out-
numbered Muslims, other government positions were distributed among
communities following a six-to-five ratio, with the advantage going to
Christian communities.[28] Political reasons have kept Lebanon from conducting any official population census since 1932, which keeps the current
sectarian distribution of the population unknown and therefore preserves
the distribution of power as it is.[29]

Sectarianism is therefore enshrined in the Lebanese political system. The
core pillar of the Lebanese political system is consociational power-sharing
based on sectarian identities, which remains the key measure of political
representation. Sectarian quotas are explicitly assigned for top government
positions, and political parties and movements are directly associated with
a specific sect, whereby the members of a party would mostly belong to
the same sect. The parliamentary electoral system is based on the sectarian allocation of parliamentary seats. The practice of voting according to
registration district rather than place of residence has prevented integration
and kept people strictly affiliated to their place of birth and thus to their
sectarian identity and community. The importance assigned to community
representation and denominational sectarianism, although instituted during
the French mandate, was exaggerated post-independence and later on
during the post-war period.[30] Sectarian identity is also the basis for personal
status. Marriage, child custody and inheritance follow the laws of each religious group, irrespective of whether citizens practise the religion to which
they are affiliated. The rites of marriage and death are under the control
of religious authorities, and those who wish to have a civil marriage are
compelled to travel abroad. Religious affiliation is descent-based and not an
optional aspect of a citizen's identity.

During the years between 1946 and 1954, Lebanon witnessed an important intellectual debate through articles, books and conferences discussing
Lebanese identity and the role that Lebanon was to play in the region.[31]
It was in this context that a liberal economic model was adopted as part
of an overarching vision that encompassed an identity and role for the
country. This vision – on which the liberal economic system in Lebanon
was based – can be summarised as follows: Lebanese society was formed
of several sectarian communities living in a country that was traditionally

considered a shelter for persecuted minorities. Located at the intersection of three continents, Lebanon had always been exposed to both western and eastern cultures.[32] This meant that freedom of movement and trade was highly compatible with the tradition of the country and its geographic location, and that governments in this region were incapable of guiding and managing the private sector. As a result, any economic model adopted by the newly independent country had to guarantee freedom of movement and exchange with the minimum restrictions possible. This vision enshrined two intertwining guiding principles: on the one hand, the need to perpetuate the sectarian system as a main pillar of Lebanese society; on the other hand, the need to stop the state intervening in the economy.[33] Ever since the creation of Lebanon, the labour movement was, therefore, hampered by two colossal obstacles: sectarian power-sharing and a free-market economy. This approach was in line with the thoughts of Lebanese political and business figures such as Michel Chiha and his followers, namely Joseph Oughourlian, who had been the mentor and chief defender of liberalism in Lebanon. Oughourlian, who later became vice-president of the Central Bank, considered the Lebanese economic model a 'historical fatality', where trade and the balance of payments were the only key factors that determined the country's economic development. He even perceived 'imports' as part of Lebanon's 'production'.[34]

Nonetheless, many opposed this vision. Georges Naqqash criticised the proponents of liberalism and promoted the intervention of the state to bring back a minimum balance between the different economic sectors. Naqqash and Maurice Jimayyil were among many others who believed in and promoted the potential of agriculture and modern industry in Lebanon.[35] Jimayyil clearly stated that Lebanon was in economic slavery. To preserve their hegemony, power elites impoverished the people and had no interest in the economic development of the country. After independence, the debate continued between proponents of economic liberalism and those who advocated reforms and the levelling of social relations among the Lebanese. Throughout the history of independent Lebanon, liberalism has been an integral part of state policies, with a brief exception during the presidential term of Fu'ad Shihab.

In the period between 1920 and 1945, Lebanon's economy performed well. Despite the decline of the silk industry, the slowing down of migration and the significant reduction in remittances, several economic activities increased. This was due to good-quality education and transport infrastructure and a surplus in the balance of payments. After 1946, the Lebanese economy was severely criticised for not achieving significant economic growth nor showing any signs of a burgeoning industry. Nevertheless, as we will see later on in this chapter, the Government did not award sufficient importance to the primary sector. Between 1939 and 1944, the economy saw a fiscal surplus cumulatively totalling LBP23 million.[36]

The commercial and financial elite immediately assumed the role of defining the economic and political future of the independent Lebanese republic as it outlined the adoption of politics favourable to triangular trade: international trade, finance and a role as the regional intermediary.[37] The influence of this elite significantly grew following the end of the French mandate and under the term of President Bishara al-Khuri. The Lebanese economy was entirely liberalised in 1948, with the easing of restrictions on foreign currencies. Although this relaxing of restrictions was only fully implemented in 1952, the foreign currency market had already spread widely since 1948. Between 1948 and 1952, laissez-faire principles were established and laws that were deemed to constrain the free market were abolished.

The liberal economic model promoting the priority of the tertiary sector, namely tourism, trade and finance, was strongly confirmed in the 1950s with the changes affecting neighbouring countries and the region in general. The onset of the oil era in the Gulf states, the occupation of Palestine, the split of Lebanon and Syria's customs authorities, along with the wave of nationalisation in many countries in the region, led to the migration of a significant part of Egypt, Syria and Iraq's commercial, financial and industrial bourgeoisie to Lebanon. This migration of business elites, in turn, strengthened the emphasis on the tertiary sector of the Lebanese economy. At the same time, a large number of Palestinian refugees were displaced to Lebanon and injected the economy with deposits into Lebanese banks. The ports of both Haifa and Alexandria were ranked behind the Port of Beirut, which became the regional centre for maritime transit. This service-oriented economy triggered a period of prosperity; however, it also exacerbated the regional disparities in the country.[38] In this context of advantageous conjuncture, it was clear that any suggestion of a long-term industrial policy as a key strategy for economic growth would have been considered inadequate. Economic liberalism suited the interests of traders, a class that appeared in the second half of the nineteenth century. Likewise, the political elite and business owners were aware of the benefits to them of the liberal economy in place. One can say that the Lebanese political system was a political and social contract, continuously renewed, that allowed the power elite to acquire economic strength.

This political landscape implied that all Lebanese governments adopted the liberal economic model without question. At this point, the monopolisation of the economy was secured, strengthening the foundation of the commercial and financial elite. The weak productive sector meant a high reliance on imports. And customs fees were imposed only as a tax-receipt guarantee, rather than for the protection of Lebanese production. At the same time monopolies in the import sector were established due to a set of regulations that paved the way for its monopolisation.[39] For instance, goods that competed with local production required an import licence from the Ministry of Economy. Only powerful traders were awarded such licences, and by 1974 the trading firms of four families accounted for almost two-thirds of all Lebanese imports from western countries. The Lebanon elite had become even more powerful.[40]

The power of the business-financial elite also clarifies the limited development of industry in the 1960s and 1970s. The fact that industry did not take a leading position in the Lebanese economy can be explained by a number of factors: the increasing linkage of the Lebanese economy to western capital, the strong competition of foreign goods and limited lending in the primary sector – all in addition to the established hegemony of the service sector and the fact that the Lebanese market was very small indeed. In fact, only light industries witnessed growth, as they only required cheap labour, as opposed to long-term investments in highly skilled salaried employees. In 1970, 67 per cent of industrial production came from food processing, textiles and building materials, which also employed almost 58 per cent of total salaried employees.[41]

In the 1960s, Yusif Sayigh noted that the financial elite was becoming the most powerful group, with a wide array of interests, including industry, tourism and real-estate development. According to Sayigh, the banking sector had become the most powerful of all sectors in the Lebanese economy. Like Kamal Hamdan and Marwan Akl,[42] Sayigh mapped out the connections of the financial elite, revealing that the major banks in the country were owned by the same small set of omnipotent bourgeois families. For example, the Sursock family, rich landlords in Beirut and important textile traders, became partners in the Banque Trad-Credit Lyonnais after independence. Banks were channelling funds into trade and real estate, while agriculture and industry lacked investment and were underdeveloped.[43]

The structure, policies and institutions of a free economy, the provision of services to the Middle East and playing the intermediary role between western and regional economies defined the economic order in Lebanon until 1958, and in a less striking way until 1975. Triggered by the interests of the power elite, these principles were translated into a model that was often referred to as the 'Merchant Republic'.[44] Through the adoption and omission of certain policies, the Government established a market with little regulation. Among the first policies adopted by the independent Lebanese state were the progressive deregulation of trade and exchange systems and the stabilisation of the Lebanese pound. The adoption of such measures put both industry and agriculture under severe pressure. The size of Lebanon and its endorsement of an open economy based on triangular trade and international services largely restricted the scope of the Government to choose macro-economic policies. In this context, few alternatives were possible outside the maintenance of a strong currency, budgetary surplus and conservative external accounts.

Against this backdrop, the growth of the industrial sector, the deteriorating living conditions of workers and the difficult economic conditions reinforced the position of the Federation of Trade Unions of Workers and Employees (FTUWE) and stimulated the workers' struggle. After independence, the FTUWE was the first federation to be established in 1944, with Mustafa al-'Aris as president. It founded the weekly paper *Hayat al-'Amil* (The Worker's Life). In 1945, a number of trade unions separated from the federation to establish the league of trade unions headed by Elias Eid. Nevertheless, both federations acted together on several issues.[45] The FTUWE considered the fight for independence as an inseparable part of the struggle for better living conditions of workers. It took part in all political actions for independence. *Hayat al-'Amil* explained in 1945 that 'the Federation is fighting to reinforce independence and the republican democratic regime in Lebanon because the freedom of the labour movement is strictly linked to independence and to this regime'.[46] Despite its condemnation of the exploitation of the bourgeoisie, the FTUWE expressed moderate positions towards the regime and did not hesitate to participate in Lebanese political life. It nominated several candidates for parliamentary elections and showed support for other progressive candidates. The FTUWE's participation in political life reflected some realism and will towards integration. The independence of Lebanon, the victory of the Allied Forces and the role of the Soviet Union in the war against Germany reinforced and strengthened the position of the FTUWE at the national level. After independence, the first and most important battle fought by the labour movement and the FTUWE, in particular, was the battle for the promulgation of the Labour Code in 1946.

The first law pertaining to labour conditions in Lebanon was the Act of 27 April 1935 addressing the work of women and children. The relation between employers and workers was regulated by the Code of Contracts and Obligations (1934), which included a specific chapter regarding contracts of employment. In 1937, Parliament amended articles 652 and 656 of the Code of Contracts dealing with the wrongful termination of contract and dismissal compensation.[47] For trade union matters, the Ottoman law of 1905 on association was used. The French mandate set specific conditions on industrial associations and issued a legal decision in 1934 to supplement the Ottoman law, by restricting membership of any occupational association to workers in the same sector.[48] At the outset of the French mandate in 1943, the newly independent Government set up the Social Affairs Services endowed with wide prerogatives concerning employment issues, mainly the questions of minimum wages and family allowances. Shortly after its establishment, the Social Affairs Services submitted to the Government a draft law concerning industrial accidents. The Lebanese industrial accident legislation (Decree No. 25) was enacted in May 1943 and gave workers considerable protection from accidents, but not from occupational disease.[49]

These ad hoc provisions for specific instances were not sufficient, and a set of permanent regulations to govern the different aspects of labour conditions was needed. The Government launched the preparation of the Labour Code. The first draft law was suggested in 1944 and was subject to several reviews and suggestions for amendment. Towards the end of 1945, the FTUWE urged the Government to provide a copy of the draft law for revision and suggestions, which they did on 23 October 1945. Earlier, the Association of Traders had reviewed and expressed their opinion on the draft law. In December 1945, the FTUWE submitted a set of comments on the draft law to the Government.[50]

The FTUWE met with the cabinet in February 1946 and reiterated its demands concerning the promulgation of the Labour Code, regulations governing trade unions and financial support of the trade unions. The parliamentary judicial committee amended the draft law. The revised law referred to 'trade unions' instead of 'associations', which the FTUWE celebrated as a significant victory. It held a demonstration and called for a general strike on 21 May 1946 to put pressure on Parliament to enact the law. Four days later, on 25 May 1946, Parliament was convened to discuss the draft legislation.[51]

The labour movement was operating on different fronts, including holding strikes at the Port of Beirut and the Banque du Syrie et Liban, on the railways and the Beirut tram system and at electricity plants and tobacco factories. In 1945, Lebanon witnessed the longest strike in the history of the labour movement. Workers of the *al-Aswaf al-Wataniyya* factory went on strike for four months, demanding the implementation of labour regulations and better working conditions. The strike of Régie tobacco workers that started on 11 June 1946 was the most violent during this period. Régie refused to start negotiations while the workers were on strike. On 27 July, a tobacco-distribution truck left the Régie premises in an attempt to break the strike. Workers lay down on the floor to block the truck from leaving. To clear the way, security forces shot at strikers and one worker, Wardi Ibrahim, was killed. She is commemorated as the first worker in Lebanon to die for the workers' cause.[52] This mobilisation created an adequate environment for the promulgation of the law, despite the differences between the FTUWE and other bodies such as the Labour Front, founded in 1946.[53] The Lebanese Parliament issued the first Labour Code on 23 September 1946. It was the first time the state officially recognised trade unions. The FTUWE considered the Labour Code as a major achievement for the labour movement, while still stressing its flaws.

The Lebanese Labour Code is composed of 114 articles relating to the type and terms of work contracts, regulations on the employment of women and children, working hours and holidays, salaries and wages, dismissal procedures and the protection of wage earners from accidents and disease. It furthermore sets out rules for the organisation of work, the establishment of an arbitration board, trade unions and the establishment of municipal employment offices. The code covers all workers except agricultural workers, domestic workers, those in liberal professions and civil servants.[54] In its first chapter, the code details the work-contract regulations, including the notice of contract severance by employer and employee, as well as regulations for the training of apprentices. In the second chapter, the Labour Code prohibits the employment of children under the age of 13. Adolescents – those between 13 and 18 years of age – can work after a medical examination but are forbidden to work in industries or jobs detrimental to their health. It also regulates the employment of women in terms of maternity leave and type of work, while prohibiting discrimination among men and women in matters including pay, working hours and promotion.

The code's third chapter establishes a working week of 48 hours and lists the required break and leave periods, including 15-days' paid leave after one year of employment. The minimum wage is determined by a commission made up of representatives of the Ministry of Labour, employers and wage earners. An important provision of the code is its stipulation of redundancy pay, which replaces some of the functions of a social security fund. Under chapter five of the law pertaining to dismissal, an employer must give workers, if they are dismissed under certain circumstances, compensation of one month's pay for each year of service. Similar compensation is made when a female worker is obliged to leave her job because she is getting married or retiring.

The code also provides for the presentation and publication of labour regulations and personal status by the employer, in addition to a set of penalties and fines for violations. According to the chapter dealing solely with the 'organisation of work', additional restrictions are used to constrain the worker from unruly and collective action: the employer will pay no compensation for dismissal if the wage earner intentionally causes material damage, violates work regulations by being absent for 7 consecutive days without a valid reason or 15 days in one year, is guilty of an offence on work premises, does not respect an arbitration decision or commits an assault on the employer.

The Lebanese Labour Code leaves little room for private rule-making or any labour-management agreement without government involvement. Under this legislation, the Government is a party to basically every labour dispute. In other words, the Government enters into detailed regulation of all phases of employment conditions and relations. The Government can intervene in compulsory arbitration at the request of both employers and employees. Employment is heavily regulated by the Government to the extent that it needs to approve the internal regulations drafted by an employer. The implementation of these internal regulations is also subject to government supervision and enforcement.[55]

The Ottoman Act of 1905 formerly governed all associations until the French mandate set special conditions for industrial associations in 1934. At this point, industrial associations had no specific prerogatives. In the Labour Code, a special chapter is dedicated to trade unions and includes detailed provisions for the functions of industrial associations and the conditions regulating their formation and management.[56]

Article 50 of the Labour Code was subject to amendment but continues to have a negative impact on trade unions and labour relations. Initially, Article 50, as it appeared in the Code in 1946, allowed the employer to dismiss any employees that were not subject to a contract or an agreement for a set period of time. Accordingly, the law did not protect workers in general, and unionists in particular, from dismissal. In the provisions of Section IV, trade unions are juridical entities and are qualified to initiate legal proceedings (Article 83). The sole objective of trade unions is to promote the interests and progress of the trade from an economic, industrial or commercial point of view. In other words, 'all political activity is prohibited to trade unions, including participation in meetings or demonstrations of a political colour' (Article 84). Trade union members may only be persons having the same occupation or similar occupations. What constitutes a similar profession or trade is specified by a ministerial order from the Ministry of Labour (Article 85).

As specified in Article 86, no 'employers' or wage earners' and salary-earners' trade union may be established except after due authorisation from the Ministry of National Economy' (currently the Ministry of Labour). Surprisingly, the authorisation required for unions is not imposed on associations and political parties, which are not required to obtain an authorisation from the Ministry of the Interior. In addition, the law does not specify a deadline for the Ministry of Labour to issue its decision regarding the authorisation. In effect, this leaves trade unions at the mercy of the minister in charge – thus, at the mercy of political will, which means that a trade union's requests may end up sitting unapproved on ministry desks.

Trade union founders are required, as per ministerial authorisation, to call for a general assembly and elect the first trade union council in the first two months of its establishment. If the elections are not conducted within this period, the authorisation is considered null and void. This period is short and overlooks the initial obstacles and bottlenecks faced by young trade unions during their founding period. It does not allow sufficient time to convince workers to join a union, to conduct initial training sessions or receive the legal advice necessary for the correct procedure for the union board election.[57]

Authorisation from the Ministry of Labour is required for the establishment of trade unions, and all their internal affairs are subject to close supervision by the Government (Article 89). Each employer and employee is free to join, choose not to become a member and to withdraw from a trade union. Trade union membership requires that the applicant must be of Lebanese nationality, possesses civil rights, carries on the profession at the time of application, must be at least 18 years old and has not been found guilty of any crime or offence (Article 91). Foreigners who satisfy these conditions except the first and who hold work permits may belong to trade unions but are not eligible to vote in union matters (Article 92). An applicant excluded or expelled from a union can appeal against the decision to the Ministry of Labour (Article 94). These articles clearly exclude foreign workers from playing any role in the labour movement.

Each union has a managerial committee of no fewer than four and not more than twelve members (Article 99). The powers of the committee and the chairman, secretary and treasurer are set out in the internal regulations (Article 102). The Government has the right to dissolve any trade union council which fails to carry out its duties and to call new elections. If the fault lies with one particular member of the council, the Government is entitled to request his or her replacement or to take legal action (Article 105). Finally, unions may merge to form federations, provided they are authorised to do so by the Ministry of Labour (Article 106). While the code stipulates the right to form federations, there is no detailing of the rights and powers of such organisations. For example, there are no provisions for collective bargaining. The word 'trade union' does not appear in the section on labour courts, and the Labour Code also does not mention the words 'strike' and 'lockout'.[58] The most striking characteristic of the law is that it limits the freedom of association. The code considers and deals with trade unions as a threat to political stability and expresses limited faith in free collective bargaining. The labour legislation provides for a very strong role for the Government and the Labour Code is in reality 'a blank check for governmental administration of all phases of labour management relations'.[59]

In addition to the limits of the Labour Code for the freedom of association in Lebanon, the Lebanese Government has only ratified the International Labour Organization's (ILO) Right to Organise and Collective Bargaining Convention of 1949 (Number 98) and has continuously refused the ratification of the ILO Freedom of Association and Protection of the Right to Organise Convention of 1948 (Number 87). Convention Number 87 pertains to human rights and the ILO incites all member states to ratify to protect human rights with respect to labour. Article 2 of Convention 87 sanctifies the right of association without pre-authorisation: 'Workers and employers, without distinction whatsoever, shall have the right to establish and, subject only to the rules of the organisation concerned, to join organisations of their own choosing without previous authorisation.' Convention 87 also provides that the procedures of union registration are limited and short, to remove conditions and procedures that might constitute an obstacle for the right of association.[60] This convention is a main pillar for the freedom of workers, but since 1948 Lebanon has abstained from ratifying while 150 states have already ratified it.[61] Pre-authorisation of unions and federations has always been an important tool for state co-optation of the labour movement, and by refusing to abide by Convention 87 the state apparatus was not willing to relinquish its control over labour power in order to maintain the sectarian-liberal regime unharmed by a strong labour opposition.

Following the promulgation of the Labour Code in 1946, the Government dissolved already existing unions, aiming to reorganise the labour movement. The Government, however, used the opportunity to build political support and only authorised trade unions and federations that were politically affiliated with the Government such as the Lebanese League of trade unions, which did not meet all requirements of authorisation at the time. The honorary president of the league of trade unions was the son of the President of the Republic, Bishara al-Khuri, a fact that strongly indicates an affiliation between the federation and the Government. In line with the policy of containing communism, the state apparatus clearly used its authorisation privileges to divide and therefore weaken the labour movement after independence.[62] Conversely, the Government did not grant authorisation to the FTUWE, which was the first federation to be formed in 1939, because of its affiliation to the LCP. The FTUWE mobilised, demanding official authorisation along with other unauthorised trade unions.

The practice of controlling the authorisation of trade unions and federations to impede and curtail the labour movement began at the beginning of the labour movement and not during the post-war period, as many observers tend to assume. The labour movement had always been subject to state intervention, which had systematically weakened its development and limited its influence since independence. More significantly, this practice of authorising federations politically affiliated to the regime did not only allow state intervention but also made the labour movement become a mere reflection of conflicts between political parties and severed it from the needs and demands of the workers it claimed to represent. Logically, political hostilities between unions and federations would intensify later on during the Lebanese Civil War, which further contributed to abate the labour movement.

The authorities resorted to using different means to weaken the FTUWE, which had to fight on many different levels, including the intervention of foreign embassies. In 1946, while the FTUWE took action to demand the promulgation of the Labour Code, a second federation, the Labour Front, was established. On 26 April 1947, the chargé d'affaires of the American Commission in Beirut sent a report to the secretary of state in Washington on trade union affairs in Lebanon. According to the report, the FTUWE was the best organised federation at the time. However, the Labour Front, a federation funded by Minister of Foreign Affairs Henri Fara'aun, was considered to be the largest federation. The League of trade unions of workers and employees, supported by former Minister of the Interior Sa'ib Salam, was expected to pose serious competition to the 'communists', according to the report.[63] These archives show the conflict between the FTUWE, considered to be a communist organisation, and the remaining federations politically allied with the Government and other foreign interests.

Without authorisation, the FTUWE was considered illegal, and on 5 January 1948 the police raided its premises and confiscated all its documents and papers. In March of the same year, the premises were raided again. On several occasions, Mustafa al-'Aris and other members of the federation were arrested for organising activities that allegedly threatened the security of the country. In 1949, a split occurred within the International Confederation of Unions (ICU). The federations that were supporting the Marshall Plan retreated and joined the International Confederation for Free Trade Unions (ICFTU). In turn, the Lebanese League of trade unions joined the ICFTU in 1949, while the FTUWE remained in the ICU. During this period, relations between the LCP and the international communist movement were consolidated. Mustafa al-'Aris and other members of the FTUWE were invited to visit the Soviet Union. The FTUWE also had a privileged relationship with the French Communist Party and the French General Confederation of Labour, which made visits to Lebanon to meet with FTUWE officials on several occasions. The FTUWE's strategies and campaigns were hence strongly influenced by the French labour movement and events in France.

From 1950, the labour movement was subject to increasing divisions. In February 1948, a group of trade unions, previously grouped under the

FTUWE, rallied under the league of trade unions of workers and employees, one of the newly authorised federations. Foreign intervention in trade union affairs increased during this period. Besides, whenever trade unions attempted to unite, the Government would intervene to preserve the existing split within the labour movement. And the more the workers' struggle intensified, the more the Government tried to repress and contain the labour movement.[64]

The waning role of the FTUWE cannot be explained only by the repression and intervention exerted by the state. After independence, the country witnessed the transformation of social structures and the development of social categories that were attached to the social order in place and opposed to all possible change. The financial elite, liberated from foreign intervention after independence, consolidated its power as it became increasingly aware of its interests and privileged economic situation. The labour market was catering to salaried employees with a bourgeois, individualistic and conservative mentality. Furthermore, the limited size of the industrial sector meant a dwindling working class. To a certain extent, these factors can explain the state's intervention in the labour movement's affairs and the weakening of the FTUWE, which was the only group capable of exerting pressure on the ruling elite.

After independence, the political power of the financial and commercial elite was fortified. The national industry that was thriving during the Second World War suffered from international competition, while in just a few years, the number of banks increased drastically. The majority of these were international banks and the financial and business elite invested mainly in the service sector. Following the Egyptian Revolution of 1952, Arab capital started to flow towards Lebanon. This phenomenon marked the Lebanese economy and exacerbated its dependence on foreign capital and its fluctuations with the international market. The increase in the number of banks, trade establishments and oil companies transformed the socio-economic structures of the country.

The Federation of united trade unions was established in 1952 and comprised five important unions: those of electricity companies, banks, railways, the Port of Beirut and the Régie. This federation was mostly composed of a privileged group of salaried employees in state-owned enterprises, and the leaders of these unions were highly ranked employees in the Lebanese administration. Like the league, the Federation of united trade unions acted against the FTUWE, as its goal was to 'save' the country from the dangers of communism. *Al-'Awasif*, a magazine published by the Federation of united trade unions, often defended the political regime and the economic system and stressed the fact that reforms should take place within the structure of the system. *Al-'Awasif* took a position against trade unions previously enrolled under the FTUWE. On the international front, *al-'Awasif* condemned the Soviet Union and supported the United States even its war in Vietnam. In under six years, trade unions were dispersed under five federations. In 1954, the league of trade unions split and two new federations were created; respectively the Federation of independent trade unions, which grouped together different professions, and the Federation of trade unions of workers and employees in North Lebanon. It is this international political conflict that was reflected on the regional level, rather than local labour issues, which steered state–labour relations between the 1950s and 1970s. In fact, on 30 April 1958, the Government authorised the establishment of the GCWL, consisting of only four right-wing bodies: the League of trade unions of workers and employees of the Lebanese Republic, the United federation of trade unions, the Federation of trade unions of North Lebanon and the Federation of independent trade unions. These were labelled the 'unionist right'. The Ministry of Social Affairs did not authorise other federations and therefore a large share of trade unions remained outside the GCWL. The confederation was inactive. The four federations rejected the implementation of any activity that related to the unification of unions while avoiding any common action with any trade union of communist affiliation. It looked like the authorisation of the confederation aimed at polarising the labour movement between left- and right-wing federations. More significantly, the four federations were not sectorial, but general or geographically based federations: the common denominator of unions within a federation was their political affiliation instead of occupation. The authorisation of general federations would intensify in the postwar period, in parallel with the intensification of state intervention and the hegemony of political parties over the confederation.

During the 1950s and 1960s, left-wing federations, excluded from the confederation, were increasingly mobilised and demanded the amendment of Article 50 of the 1946 Labour Code. As discussed earlier, Article 50 gave the employer the right to dismiss workers for any reason and with short notice. The workers demanded a wage increase, the establishment of a social security fund, paid holidays, the reduction of working hours, and the right of workers to establish labour unions without government intervention.[65] During this period, the labour movement was active on the political front as well as in demanding socio-economic rights and public freedom, and working for the unity and common action of the labour movement. It is noteworthy that an exceptional reformist period occurred between 1958 and 1964 during which President Fu'ad Shihab proclaimed explicit objectives pertaining to the establishment and consolidation of state institutions, with the purpose of achieving economic and social development. This was the only period in the history of Lebanon when a government had a major national objective of economic and social development. Seminal civil-service, planning and infrastructure institutions were established during the term of Fu'ad Shihab. The Banque du Liban, the central bank of Lebanon, was established in 1964, and the dissemination of national accounts data began in the same year. Public spending on education was increased and a draft law relating to social security was passed. Physical infrastructure was upgraded, notably in rural areas.[66]

The development strategy implemented under Shihab was based on an in-depth survey of socio-economic conditions in the different regions of Lebanon conducted in 1959 by a French consultancy firm (IRFED) commissioned by the Government.[67] Poverty mapping showed a concentration of pockets of poverty in the north of the country and the Bekaa (Akkar, Dunniya and Hermel), as well as in parts of South Lebanon.[68] In addition, belts of poverty were swelling in Beirut and Tripoli due to an influx of the poor from rural regions. The situation was putting at risk and endangering the national unity and social cohesion of the country, thus requiring special attention from the various governments during Shihab's presidency. The creation of a Social Development Office was a landmark and more importantly, a cornerstone for the implementation of social policies. However, the Government barely intervened in the regulation of the market despite the 1959 IRFED mission findings and the Government's vision. In fact, the infrastructure upgrading and Shibab's achievements of setting up institutions created an adequate framework for the healthy functioning of the market.[69]

Unlike the terms of Bishara al-Khuri and Kamil Sham'un, that of President Fu'ad Shihab (1958–64) prioritised socio-economic development projects. In brief, he expanded the public sector and education, extended healthcare provision to rural areas, and launched infrastructure projects. Between 1957 and 1964, public expenditure surged, indicating the involvement of the state in socio-economic development, such as the establishment of the National Social Security Fund (NSSF).[70] In a speech delivered on 22 November 1962, Shihab clearly linked socio-economic development to nation-building. 'The development project that is taking place in the economic and social sectors is seen not only as a way to raise the standard of living of each individual but also to ground all Lebanese in a single society on which national unity is based – not as much on the basis of coexistence or the association of different parts of the population but rather on people and to make them want to remain loyal to the country.'[71]

Amid government and foreign intervention, the labour movement carried on its struggle for better socio-economic conditions, despite witnessing divisions and interventions from the Government as well as the ICFTU.[72] Following a period of relative stagnation, after 1960 the labour movement

launched a number of large-scale mobilisations at different levels. The
action for socio-economic demands was well organised and there was coordination between unions. An organisational movement emerged and led to
the setting-up of trade union meetings to examine worker and union issues.
The Group of Unions organised a seminal meeting on 18 October 1959,
gathering representatives from the Ministry of Labour, other federations
and the unions grouped under the Group of Unions. Another consultative
meeting was organised a month later on 18–19 November 1959, and this
meeting included the submission of a report on the NSSF draft law and the
amendment of the Labour Code.[73]

With the increasingly difficult conditions for workers, the Group of
Unions organised a one-month union conference in February 1962. The
conference included 60 out of 101 authorised unions with 90 delegates
representing 60,000 wage earners. This conference was the first of its kind
in post-independence Lebanon and stressed the need for the promulgation
of the NSSF law and the amendment of the Labour Code, especially Article
50. The conference also stressed the urgency for extending the legislation
to include agricultural workers, who were excluded from the Labour Code
of 1946 and had no rights of association. The conference called upon all
participants, as well as non-participating federations, and all workers to
undertake joint union action to achieve these objectives.

The bustling activity of trade unions during this period reflected the
intensified conflict between left-wing and loyalist parties. In order to
counter the work of loyalist trade unions, the left-wing trade unions
grouped under the Workers' Liberation Front (WLF).[74] In 1962, the
Minister of the Interior, Kamal Junblat, Head of the Progressive Socialist
Party (PSP), awarded the new WLF an official authorisation. During this
period, the WLF fought for socio-economic demands but was also significantly involved in the political struggle of leftist parties, especially the LCP
and the PSP. In 1965, the WLF, along with the parties of the Liberation
Front and the Group of Independent Unions, organised a large protest,
which led to the promulgation of the law pertaining to end-of-service compensation for private-sector workers.

Between 1960 and 1961, the labour movement called for twenty-nine
strikes, mostly demanding wage increases and the amendment and implementation of labour provisions and social safety nets.[75] As a result, 1961
saw the first wage increase since 1944, and in 1965 another wage increase
was declared.[76] Between 1960 and 1966, the union movement focused on
socio-economic issues and labour provisions, calling for 61 strikes, 46 of
which were in the industrial sector and 15 in the service sector. The key
achievements of the labour movement during this period were the promulgation of the NSSF law in 1963 and the Agreement, Conciliation and

Arbitration Act of 1964. According to Albert Mansour, a significant share of strikes between 1954 and 1977 (38 out of 95) were successful.[77]

The labour movement developed a more political aspect, especially after the Israeli attack on Beirut's airport in 1968 and the events of 23 April 1969.[78] During this period, the country remained without a government for six months and the labour movement took action to demand the formation of a government, the amendment of the Labour Code – mainly Articles 13, 40, 50, and 74 – the authorisation of a new trade union structure and the participation of unions in government social institutions and socio-economic legislation.[79] In 1966, the Ministry of Social Affairs authorised five new federations, which adhered to the GCWL: the FTUWE and the federations of trade unions of workers and employees of oil companies, workers and employees in South Lebanon, workers in independent authorities and private and public institutions and workers in independent authorities. The authorisation of a left-wing federation, namely the FTUWE, was part of a general policy that aimed to integrate the Lebanese left in the system, as long as it did not constitute a serious danger to it. The authorisation of the LCP in 1970 fell under the same strategy.[80] This new form of solidarity and unity of the labour movement did not flatten the differences among federations, which in fact reflected the complexity and contradictions of Lebanese society. The coexistence of different federations within the GCWL showed a will for cooperation and integration. The reaction of the GCWL to the serious events that shook Lebanon was rather timid. The federations in the GCWL took no position with regard to the Palestinian problem apart from the FTUWE and the national Federation of trade unions of South Lebanon. The most powerful trade unions represented a privileged category of salaried employees who were motivated, not by their place in the economic process, but by their familial and sectarian identities. Moreover, a large number of salaried workers still did not have the right to form a trade union (workers in agriculture and on zero-hours contracts and foreign and domestic workers). Hence, the actual inclination and movement towards unity within the labour movement remained partial and only targeted a fraction of salaried workers. In 1970, all five federations that had remained outside the GCWL rallied under its umbrella. From that day onwards, the GCWL became the main representative of trade unions in Lebanon. The charter of the GCWL enacted in 1970 is still functional today and has not been amended, although it was meant to be temporary, 'for a period of one year during which a new structure will be put in place based on sectorial pillars that reflect the economic sectors of the country'. These regulations were controversial and considered to be behind the weakening of the confederation. While many attempts to reform the internal regulations were made after the 1960s by the FTUWE, many obstacles hindered these efforts and the confederation remains stagnant to this day. The GCWL charter is composed of 41 articles, and as set out in Article 12, the GCWL is composed of four bodies. The executive council is an administrative body that manages the GCWL and takes executive decisions on matters including agreements, budget, demonstrations and calls for industrial action. The executive council is composed of two representatives for every member federation (Articles 13–20). The second body is the executive bureau, composed of twelve members elected by the executive council for a four-year term. The president of the executive bureau is the official spokesperson of the GCWL and chairs all meetings of the executive council, executive bureau and the general assembly (Articles 21–25). The CR is composed of four representatives assigned by each member federation. It holds the legislative power and can veto any decision taken by the executive council (Articles 26–35). It is important to note that the representatives of each federation within the GCWL are appointed by the federation itself and are not elected democratically. Moreover, each federation has the same number of representatives and votes regardless of its size. In other words, a federation with 500 members has the same number of representatives, and therefore votes, as a federation with 5,000 members. The general assembly is the fourth and highest authority and is composed of the executive council, the executive bureau, the president and secretary-general of every member federation, plus the president and secretary-general of every trade union that falls under any member federation (Articles 36–40). This organisational structure is prone to political intervention via vote engineering, which partially explains the proliferation of federations mainly after the war. At the founding stage, this structure was initially set up to actively tame conflicts between rival federations in terms of political affiliations, or even ideological stance. However, this structure lacked two key democratic features. First, the lower body voting for the superior one was not applied (the CR does not elect the executive council). Secondly, the proportional representation of federations according to the total number of members was also not applied (today, the size of federations varies between a few hundred and 9,000 members). This structure impacted not only the internal relations among federations but also the type of decisions taken by the confederation, as well as their enforcement. Decisions taken by the executive council might not reflect the position of federations, which could have negative repercussions for the decisions of the GCWL. Furthermore, the GCWL suffered from limited funding as sparse membership fees were collected from member federations. The confederation mainly relied on the assistance of the Government and foreign institutions, which likely has had negative repercussions and implications for the independence of the labour movement. Towards the end of the 1980s, several amendment projects were suggested by different bodies

– including proposals by the Federation of united trade unions and the national Federation of trade unions – to amend the GCWL charter. Nevertheless, none of these initiatives went through, and all attempts at reform were sabotaged by members of the confederation and the Ministry of Labour in order to get a better stranglehold on the confederation. A snapshot of the evolution of trade unions during the pre-war period shows that the labour movement was fragmented and scattered. Several small trade unions represented the same profession. The evolution of trade unions reflects the transformation in the socio-economic structures marked by the predominance of the service sector. Between 1956 and 1966, the number of trade unions increased from 72 to 117. The annual increase in trade unions was 5 per cent and the annual increase of unionised members for the same period 9 per cent. In 1966, the average number of members per union was a mere 298.[81] Another key aspect of the labour movement that should be examined is the share of unionised workers. Based on the available data, this was in decline – it stood at 20.6 per cent in 1960 and 22.3 per cent in 1965. These figures only partially describe the situation, as during this period, a large number of Syrian and Palestinian labourers worked in the industrial and informal sectors without being registered at the Ministry of Social Affairs or the NSSF. When taken into account, the number of foreign workers would decrease the share of unionised workers.[82] According to a survey conducted among wage earners in 1986, the number of unionised workers during the war was estimated at 14 per cent. In the absence of official data on the labour force and trade unions during this period, this estimate seems reasonable. During the 1975–90 war, the share of unionised workers was expected to have decreased.[83] Another feature of the labour movement is the distribution of members by trade union. Which were the largest trade unions, and to what sector did they belong? In the pre-war period, five main trade unions represented 30.7 per cent of total union members. Out of the largest 5 unions, 3 representing workers in the industrial sector comprised 20 per cent of total union membership.[84] The other two main trade unions respectively represented employees of the Central Bank (5 per cent) and Middle East Airlines (5.69 per cent). Conversely, more than 100 trade unions comprised 56 per cent of total members. These small trade unions, of around 100 members each, show the fragmentation of the labour movement.[85]

How can trade unions with such limited membership constitute a pressure group? And how can such small bodies elaborate coherent strategies towards the achievement of national demands? The labour movement in the pre-war period had rarely staged protests, and trade union demands in Lebanon narrowly focused on a call for economic changes and did not go beyond to include larger transformative demands. Looking beyond the

Table 1 Share of trade union members out of total membership (%), 1965

Name of trade union	Members (%)
Workers and employees in the textile industries and trade	10.18
Workers and employees of Tobacco Régie	6.25
Workers and employees of Middle East Airlines	5.69
Employees of the Central Bank	5.00
Workers and employees of railway companies	3.45
Workers and employees in hotels, cafés and restaurants	2.80
Teachers in private schools	2.78
Workers in and employees of hotels and restaurants	2.69
Employees of the Port of Beirut	2.30
Engineers and metalworkers	2.10
Remaining 107 trade unions	56.60
Total	100

Source: Younes, *Histoire et structure du mouvement syndical au Liban.*

unions' main characteristics, the distribution of trade unions among the different federations also helps to examine the political significance of the actions and behaviour of trade unions. In fact, the consortium of trade unions under one particular federation reflects a specific attitude and a strategic choice. The GCWL was established in 1958, composed of only three authorised federations: the GCWL and the federations of united syndicates and North Lebanon. It took until May 1970 to subsume all trade union federations under the GCWL.[86] In the three years between 1972 and 1975, the demands of the labour movement focused on increasing wages, amending the NSSF law and Article 50 of the Labour Code. The mobilisation of workers in the pre-war period partly stemmed from the relatively large industrial sector that drastically dwindled after the war.[87] In 1970, the service sector comprised 41 per cent of wage earners, trade 15 per cent, industry 19 per cent, construction 7 per cent and agriculture 19 per cent. During this period, the activity rate was as low as 45 per cent.[88] The male participation rate stood at 75 per cent while the female participation rate was a mere 15 per cent. At the time, only 30 per cent of women could read and write and just 1 per cent of women were university graduates. A series of protests were organised by industrial workers demanding legislation regulating working hours, a minimum wage, equal pay for men and women, family allowances, maternity and sick leave, the right to trade union organisation, recognition of shop-floor committees, opposition to arbitrary lay-offs, and National Social Security Fund coverage for agricultural workers. The strike of the Ghandour factory workers constituted the crowning point of this struggle. In November 1972, around 1,200 unionised workers went on strike demanding a wage increase, equal pay, the recognition of shop-floor committees and the right to trade union organisation.[89] Security forces intervened using violence, resulting in the death of two workers[90] as well as many injuries and the arrest of many others. Two months later, the Government took similar violent measures against demonstrations by tobacco workers. On 24 January 1973, two agricultural workers were killed and several injured in a demonstration of tobacco workers in Nabatiya.[91] And in March 1975, the politician and activist Ma'ruf Sa'd was killed during a protest by fishermen against the fishing enterprise Proteine, which was monopolising fishing in Saida. In 1973, a campaign began for the amendment of Article 50 of the Labour Code. In August 1973, a general strike was declared against inflation and increased prices. At this point, right-wing federations within the GCWL relied on the promises of the Government for the provision of workers' demands. As a result, a general strike was postponed five times between September 1973 and April 1974 by the GCWL due to the opposition of right-wing federations. In response, the left-wing national Federation of workers and employees organised a demonstration on 27 March 1974, with 50,000 workers participating prior to the general strike called for 2 April 1974. Following this general strike, the Government amended Article 50 of the Labour Code. This was achieved after an agreement between the Government and the GCWL, which entailed an amendment to Article 50 and changes to Decree 34: an increase in the minimum wage and a 10 per cent wage increase for those under 20 years of age, plus improved family allowances. Article 50 was revised by Decree No. 9640 of 1975, which stipulates that the 'dismissal of the members of a trade union council, duly elected, shall depend, during the period of their tenure, on recourse to the competent Conciliation Board'. The protection of unionists, therefore, remained limited to the elected board members of unions licensed by the Ministry of Labour. Consequently, the Labour Code does not protect union leaders during the founding period – the period between the application for establishing a union and the elections of the trade union CR following the authorisation from the Ministry of Labour. This period is critical and usually the time when unionists need protection the most as unions are often established when conflicts arise between workers and employers. Thus, freedom of association continued to be threatened despite the amendment of Article 50, especially as the flawed code did not prevent employers intervening during a trade union's founding period and allowed for the dismissal of workers or their forced resignation.[92] With the outbreak of civil war in 1975, the labour movement entered a new phase.

Workers and warlords

Lebanon enjoyed relative peace following its independence from France in 1943. From 1975, this changed, as the country experienced a 15-year civil war and several Israeli invasions. There are various approaches to the causes of the civil war, including exploring sectarian tensions, socio-economic conditions and the Palestinian–Israeli conflict, as well as the intervention of other countries. Although the war ended in 1990 with the Ta'if Agreement, Israel retained a presence in South Lebanon until 2000, as did the Syrian army until 2005. The civil war left over 150,000 dead and 17,000 missing and also destroyed much of the infrastructure and social services of the pre-war era.

During the civil-war phase, the state was weak but managed to maintain a functioning central authority and administration. While most tax revenues, notably customs duties, were controlled by militias, the Government managed to regularly pay its public-sector employees and to maintain wheat and fuel subsidies. In general, private enterprises continued to operate normally, except during intense and widespread warfare. During the 15 years of conflict, the economy performed relatively well due to its remarkable capacity to adjust to unstable conditions. According to Toufic Gaspard, 'the laissez-faire system did largely contribute to maintaining economic activity and exchange with minimal disruption and to the regular supply of commodities and the virtual absence of shortages'.[93] Economic output fell in 1976 to one-third of its level in 1974, when the fighting spread to many parts of the country. The second drop in output occurred in 1982, in the wake of the Israeli invasion; falling by 30 per cent followed by another 15 per cent reduction. In 1988–90, a third drop plunged the economic output to half of its average in 1987, when intensive fighting devastated the country. During the war, the industrial sector was considerably more resilient and flexible. Arab markets were the main destination of industrial-sector exports. A survey of Lebanese industry in 1980 showed that 20 per cent of industrial enterprises were established in 1975, of which 40 per cent were dealing with chemicals, metal and engineering products, and electricity. By 1985, mechanisation had increased by 50 per cent compared to 1971–73. The most dramatic phenomenon of the economy during the war was the exchange rate. From 1948 until 1993, the Lebanese pound followed a floating exchange rate. However, over the years 1986–87, the exchange rate depreciated by a yearly average of 80 per cent.[94] In the labour market, employment was marred by stagnation. Between 1974 and 1987, some studies estimated that employment in the private sector increased by only 11 per cent. At the same time, labour emigration increased, accompanied by an influx of unskilled foreign labour, mostly Arab and Asian workers. During this period salaries dwindled, partially due to lower levels of productivity and employers' attempts to maintain profit levels. In turn, this led to increased working hours and a rise in emigration overseas in search of work. A review of the statements of the GCWL during the war allows for an analysis of the evolution of demands in terms of types, themes and recurrence. During the civil war, the call for wage increases was predominant: the GCWL requested this every year during the war. However, this demand seemed to mature with time, as the GCWL seemed to become increasingly aware of the factors and elements determining wage value. Wage increases were no longer sufficient to improve workers' living conditions, and hence the GCWL eventually also requested the amendment of taxation on earnings, a reduction in doctors' fees, and state bread subsidies. In 1981, the GCWL called for the formation of a tripartite committee to monitor the consumer price index made up of representatives of employers, the state and the workers. The confederation demanded the linking of salaries to the consumer price index. With increasing inflation, in 1984 the confederation demanded that wages be linked to the value of the Lebanese pound and in 1985 insisted on the adoption of an indexed salary scale. In 1986, the GCWL demanded the control of foreign currencies and in 1987 measures to strengthen the Lebanese pound. After the Ta'if Agreement, the GCWL voiced successive demands for wage increases, and in 1992 called out the ineffectiveness of sporadic interventions and for the first time voiced the need for a more structured state policy with regard to salaries. The economic demands of the GCWL can best be characterised as redundant and repetitive, which reflects the stagnation of the economic situation and its recurrent crises. It also highlights the incapacity of the state and the ruling elite, and points to the inefficiency of partial solutions. Moreover, repeating the same demands could also point to their lack of efficiency and competence. Also, the GCWL made economic demands that targeted a wide range of the population. The detrimental conditions during the civil war widened the span of these demands, that went on to involve rents, the consumption of basic goods and services, water, public transport, power, education and toxic waste. It was also typical for the political demands of the GCWL to be moderate and timidly worded. Political demands and protestation were usually expressed in a careful tone. Furthermore, some memorandums praised political figures. The confederation was not able to take a clear stance regarding any political party or militia during the civil war years. The different political and sectarian affiliations of its members hampered the adoption of a unified political vision. The confederation's political demands tackled the general situation during the war without delving into the specificities of events. Unable to clearly formulate political demands, the confederation resorted to overall moderate, neutral and often vague positions. The confederation did not oppose the political system in place, despite the failing state during the war. It complained about and highlighted the lack of democratic practice. In a document issued in 1983, the GCWL presented its position regarding the political situation based on general principles – the independence and sovereignty of Lebanon, liberation of the territory from Israeli occupation, the unity of the country, the withdrawal of foreign armies, the rejection of sectarianism, justice and freedom of trade unions. It also stressed the need for constitutional reforms, mainly the promulgation of a new electoral law and the secularisation of the state.[95] Summing up, the confederation voiced reticent political demands that can best be labelled as 'cautiously reformist'. At the beginning of 1975, the GCWL expressed demands related to housing, education, cooperatives, taxation on revenue and a wage increase. It also condemned the Israeli aggression on South Lebanon, but otherwise remained mostly silent during the rest of the year. During the two first years of the conflict, the GCWL did not undertake any action and it was the FTUWE that stepped in and expressed workers' demands by organising conferences and meetings. The president of the FTUWE, Elias Haber, declared his support for the Palestinian cause, contrary to the reserved position of the GCWL.[96] In November 1976, the Arab Deterrence Forces (ADF) entered Lebanon and a ceasefire was declared. The prime minister formed a technocratic cabinet that quickly started designing reconstruction plans. Subsequently, the GCWL considered repairing its premises, and its secretary-general requested that the Government increase its annual contribution threefold.[97] During that year, the GCWL elected Georges Saqr as president, and his first declarations were about the need for trade union reorganisation. The short respite from war in 1977 triggered no additional action or mobilisation. The period between 1977 and 1983 was characterised by a weakened discourse. Trade unions were subject to restrictions caused by the war in general and the rule of militias in particular. The GCWL had a delayed reaction to the Israeli invasion that took place in March 1978 – it took 15 days following the invasion for the GCWL to condemn the Israeli occupation. The delay was due to the lack of agreement within the executive bureau regarding the stance of the confederation. In fact, the condemnation of the Israeli invasion created internal divisions within the confederation. On 9 May 1978, the GCWL's president, Georges Saqr, accompanied by trade union leaders, met with Bashir Jimayyil of the Phalanges Party, which was allied with Israel. In reaction to this meeting, ten federations rallied around Antoine Bishara, president of the Federation of trade unions of independent authorities and public institutions, and boycotted the GCWL meeting arranged for the following day. The ten federations organised a meeting outside the GCWL premises, where Halim Matar, heading up the federation of print workers, requested the resignation of Georges Saqr. Following these internal divisions, the GCWL mollified its positions during that year. The political incompatibility between the members of the GCWL exacerbated the already timid and slow positions of the GCWL, which limited its discourse in support of the displaced workers from South Lebanon following the Israeli aggression.

During the war, the GCWL frequently met with militia leaders, and its relation to militias was reinforced in the 1980s. In preparation for a strike, meetings with the leader of the Lebanese Forces, Bashir Jimayyil, and to Nabih Birri, leader of the Amal Movement, reflected the role of militias in shaping the economic situation of the country. The Lebanese Front (LF) and the Lebanese National Movement invited the GCWL to a series of meetings to discuss its demands regarding the NSSF.[98] During this period, newspapers started to mention the socio-economic role of militias and the political affiliation of trade union leaders. In 1982, the collaboration between Christian right-wing trade unions and Christian militias became obvious. Christian militias participated in the management of the economic crisis. Newspapers emphasised the role of Bashir Jimayyil in the publication of the consumer price index.[99] The right-wing Lebanese Forces militia, with increasing power, decided, through a coordination committee, to take part in the publication of the official consumer price index, which constituted the key indicator that framed the problem of wages losing their value and the ensuing need for their indexation. Left-wing federations and political parties protested against the increasing intervention of the Lebanese Forces in the GCWL. In April 1982, the Communist Labour Organisation complained of the 'attempt of certain parties of known affiliations, to put the decisions of the GCWL under the authority of isolationist forces, precisely under the authority of Bashir Jimayyil'.[100] In reaction, eighteen federations rallied under the GCWL Secretary-General Tufiq abu Khalil and threatened to leave the confederation. Similarly, federations representing Christian areas threatened to leave the GCWL. As a result, the GCWL became more fragile and less radical in its position. Regardless of inflation and its catastrophic impact on wages, the position, demands and actions of the confederation were steered by the conflict between political forces. During the civil war, the confederation was subject to additional political intervention and polarisation, which were already in place before the outbreak of the war.

With the increasing power of right-wing Christian parties, the confederation, with a Christian president at the wheel, increased their visits to Christian leaders. On the death of Pierre Jimayyil, founder of the Phalanges Party, in 1984, the GCWL suspended the meeting of its executive council and issued a memorandum that qualified Jimayyil as a 'symbol of national struggle ... [who] ... fought throughout his life for independence, national unity, charity, and forgiveness'. After a meeting with the Lebanese Forces in 1985, the confederation issued a memorandum that praised Elias Hobayka, commander-in-chief of the Lebanese Forces. The memorandum expressed the confederation's satisfaction with the freedom enjoyed at trade-union level in the Christian region.[101]

The slogans and declarations of Antoine Bishara, however, did not reflect the relationship between the confederation and the Lebanese Forces. Bishara reiterated the political independence of the confederation and called for the closure of illegal ports, which were controlled by Christian militias. Following the Ta'if Agreement in 1990, the confederation distinctly supported the disbanding of all militias. The attitude of the confederation towards militias was both a reflection of sectarian affiliations and also elasticity of positions. In fact, the confederation was characterised by the fact that it did not question the political and economic system in place. Finally, it was typical for the GCWL to react to events with either a delayed or no response. During the war, the confederation refrained from reacting to several important political events, including the demonstration of fishermen in Saida in 1975, the outbreak of war in April 1975, the assassination of political figures, militia wars, reconciliation summits and the agreement of 17 May 1983. During the civil war, the confederation communicated a clear position regarding three main events: the 1978 Israeli invasion, the second Israeli invasion that took place in 1982, and the intra-militia war of the Lebanese Forces. However, the confederation's standpoints were marked by delays caused by the disagreement of left- and right-wing federations within the confederation regarding the Syrian presence in Lebanon and the Israeli occupation.

Between 1983 and 1986, the economic situation was critical: GDP sharply declined and imports skyrocketed, making up to 80 per cent of goods. The country witnessed a deficit in both budget and balance of payments. The national currency collapsed. The stark economic situation had harsh repercussions for living conditions. Prices surged and purchasing power decreased sharply. The reaction of the GCWL was limited to reaching out to officials, making demands and threatening strike action. In 1983, the foremost demand of the GCWL was to be included in the decision-making concerning economic, social and national policies. The GCWL's political standpoints were inconsistent that year. On 2 February 1982, Antoine Bishara, now president of the GCWL, discussed the 'political identity' of the GCWL and the legitimacy of its participation in national decisions. Nonetheless, the GCWL remained silent regarding the 17 May Agreement and the strife between Christians and Druze, and the related massacres taking place in the Shouf area. Instead, the GCWL seemed to focus on its internal organisation. The multitude of affiliations within the

GCWL spawned the lack of a clear political stand on critical occurrences shaping the political arena.[102]

In 1984, the GCWL focused on the improvement of living conditions, including demands concerning power cuts and high school tuition fees. The confederation addressed inflation for the first time and criticised state economic policies. During this year, the 17 May Agreement was revoked and a reconciliation conference took place in Switzerland. Subsequently, Rashid Karami formed a cabinet in April 1984. While political instability rose in 1985, the GCWL remained mostly silent. Its political demands were scant and limited to the condemnation of the Israeli occupation. In fact, its executive council did not meet during the two months of June and July 1985. In an interview conducted by the daily *al-Anwar* newspaper, Bishara explained the apathy of the GCWL: 'the sectarian structure [of the GCWL] hampers the outbreak of a real revolution'.[103]

In 1986, the Lebanese State had lost all control amid inter-militia fighting. In March 1986, the GCWL demanded 'the cessation of an 11-year-long war between brothers'.[104] The GCWL continuously demanded the end of hostilities and was part of an anti-war movement that managed to stage several strikes and demonstrations between 1986 and 1988. When civil war had first broken out, the confederation took a political stand and immediately denounced the war and expressed views vis-à-vis its causes. It issued several declarations that mainly rejected the use of violence to settle political issues. The statements of the confederation explained that the Lebanese conflict was due to a weak political structure, the stagnation of the economic system and the misuse of democracy, as well as the detrimental role of political sectarianism. It also stressed the necessity to give priority to the support of South Lebanon in its resistance against Israeli aggression.

The discourse of the confederation during the early years of the war clearly condemned the sectarian strife.[105] As the conflict continued, the confederation's clear stance changed. Between 1977 and 1983, the confederation drifted towards apolitical positions. For instance, the General Union Conference organised in 1980 was entitled 'against high prices and for wage increase' and strictly focused on economic demands concerning the working and living conditions of workers without tackling the political situation.[106] The period 1984–87 witnessed renewed action and resistance to war from civil society, which culminated in a National Trade Unions Conference in May 1987 with the title 'No to war, yes to understanding, no to hunger, yes to the legitimate living conditions demands'. Several bodies participated in the conference, including civil society organisations, federations, teachers' unions and leagues of public school teachers and employees.[107] As can be seen in the collected archives of Elias Haber, not all members of the GCWL supported the unconditional cessation of war, which hampered the clear position of the GCWL. Once again, the confederation's structure and the resulting difficult decision-making process paralysed the GCWL and neutralised its decisions, resulting in a reduction of its activities and impact.[108] The anti-war mobilisation was organised under difficult security conditions whereby GCWL members were unable to meet in one place. Meetings would be held at both the east and west ends of the physically divided capital, while the president of the GCWL would coordinate among the executive members. These strenuous efforts to meet under very difficult circumstances, however, reflect the will of the GCWL for action. It also indicates a difficult and challenging decision-making process.[109]

On 22 June 1986, GCWL President Antoine Bishara[110] declared July to be a 'month of popular struggle to save Lebanon from war and hunger'.[111] He declared the fight against poverty and hunger went hand-in-hand with the denunciation of sectarianism and the rule of militias. The statement called for the cessation of the civil war and denounced the banking sector for its monopolies and speculation. The confederation decided to carry out a three-week mobilisation in July with incremental escalation. On 3 July 1986, a general national strike was staged and a week later demonstrations were organised in different regions. However, on 16 July, one day before popular protests were to take place at the national level, the GCWL backed down. On 17 July, despite the retreat of the GCWL, demonstrations took place in different regions without any escalation, contrary to statements by the confederation warning of risks. The GCWL's executive council explained in its statement that it had received threats concerning the planned demonstrations in Beirut, which it decided to act upon. It declared that every region should independently decide whether to participate in the demonstrations.[112]

Although of limited impact, the 1986 mobilisation witnessed new coordination between civil society organisations and the GCWL. This mobilisation brought together socio-economic demands and calls for an end to the war. Despite internal organisational difficulties and complications due to the conflict, this mobilisation was the first to include the different regions and sects of the country since the outbreak of war. During that year, the GCWL was subject to increasing political intervention. A meeting was held between the GCWL and Georges Sa'ada, then president of the Phalanges Party, to evaluate the results of the sit-in organised for 9 July 1986.[113] In October, the GCWL presented its projects to Maronite deputies and in November it informed the Lebanese Front of its activities.[114] During this period, confederation meetings took place across the demarcation lines and were subject to increasing intervention by militias. On 19 November 1986, the confederation issued a memorandum declaring 'the State is at the same time absent and present, responsible and irresponsible'.

In 1987, the confederation was more present and active, declaring a series of demands pertaining to the increase in treasury bonds, rents of maritime property and the adoption of austerity plans. It also called for better working conditions for teachers, agricultural workers and employees of Middle East Airlines. Political demands became more radical, with the GCWL demanding the closure of illegal ports, elimination of illegal taxation and the opening of passages between divided areas. In May 1987, the first National Trade Unions Conference issued a set of decisions on national, economic, financial, monetary and social issues. During this time, the GCWL plainly expressed its concerns for state unity and national peace, and called for a solution to the political vacuum following the assassination on 1 June 1987 of the resigned Prime Minister Rashid Karami. The truce between militias in tandem with the worsening economic situation opened a space for the GCWL to step up and actively voice a series of demands. The political crisis and the long-lasting economic crisis triggered large popular protests along with strikes and sit-ins in July 1987.

On 30 September 1987, a follow-up National Union Conference was organised under the heading 'Against hunger, and for a free, independent, united and sovereign country that provides democracy, decent life, and social justice'. The conference called for demonstrations in all Lebanese regions on 15 October. Two marches, one advancing from East Beirut and another from West Beirut, met and gathered together in front of Parliament. The conference had called for a general strike on 5 November against the collapse of the national currency, demanding its protection. The strike was accompanied by large demonstrations in different regions, but mainly in the capital, where protesters from East and West Beirut again gathered mid-way. Several factors can explain the exceptional open strike and nationwide protests. Economically, the devaluation of the national currency reached its peak in 1987, coupled with 400 per cent inflation and a complete collapse of purchasing power. Devaluation of the national currency and skyrocketing inflation affected all segments of society – wage earners, employers, the self-employed and business owners – which triggered urgent cooperation between the GCWL, professional orders and business associations. Moreover, the organisation of strikes and protests was taking place amid a splintering of different militias across regions, which lessened their control of GCWL action and allowed, in turn, for the emergence of independent political action. At the government level, a deadlock between President of the Republic Amin Jimayyil and Prime Minister Omar Karami halted any possible negotiations between the labour movement and the Government, which left the labour movement with one action – to take the streets. However, on 9 November, the confederation abruptly suspended the strike, despite massive nationwide participation. The statement issued by the conference calling off the open-ended strike was ambiguous. It said that the strike was cancelled as it had achieved some of its secondary demands, even though its main demands focused on the protection of the national currency. It also explained that the strike had to be suspended to avoid its politicisation by any political party.

This sudden cancellation was also caused by a lack of agreement among conference stakeholders on a direct and clear political message for the mobilisation and their inability to confront the ruling militias. The political conflict and the rule of the militias were difficult matters for the conference to criticise and condemn. In fact, the statement failed to mention the pressure exerted by the militias; direct pressure to suspend the strikes expressed at meetings between militia leaders and representatives of the GCWL, reversing the strike in certain regions under militia control by forcing enterprises to resume work, and through media campaigns that criticised the political objectives of the strike.

Another factor that might explain why the strike was called off were the divergent demands among the GCWL leadership, elections for which had been suspended since the beginning of the war, and protesters. According to the president of the GCWL at the time, the confederation 'was demanding reform while people wanted change'.[115] In reality, the confederation was not prepared to undertake the organisation and coordination of nationwide actions, and its role was limited to high-level meetings – short of any general assembly meetings or regional and local coordination meetings. Regardless of the limited organisation, according to most newspapers the level of strike participation was very high – a fact that may allude to the intensity of the popular movement that had compensated for the lack of organisation. It looked as if the sudden degradation of living conditions owing to devaluation and inflation had pushed the confederation into taking these needed actions without being ready on the organisational level, or even at the political level. Nevertheless, organisation was needed to be able to cope with the militias' opposition to the strike.

The GCWL's difficult decision-making and its paralysis in dealing with the political component of drumming up support is one of the key factors that explain the limited impact of this mobilisation. In fact, the cancellation of the strike led to instant protests expressing opposition to the political pressure on stakeholders to call it off. Demonstrations took place in different Lebanese regions, mainly Beirut, where more than 60,000 demonstrators from East and West Beirut converged. The protests point out a will to continue the strike while at the same time the incapacity to do so. Despite its disappointments in 1987, in 1988 the confederation repeated its demands for a wage increase, improvement of the NSSF, price controls and the creation of an emergency economic and social committee. It stressed the importance of the guarantee of sovereignty, the achievement of national unity and the need for presidential elections. The confederation protested against the Syrian intervention to settle the intensifying conflict between the two political parties Hezbollah and Amal and the failure to elect a president following the end of Jimayyil's term. The confederation remained silent and took no standpoint regarding the appointment of General Michel Aoun as prime minister and interim president on 22 September, in parallel to the Government of Salim al-Hoss. Starting on 23 September, the meetings of the executive council were suspended. On 11 November, GCWL issued a memorandum that insisted on the importance of sovereignty and condemned the division of the country.

In 1989, the GCWL followed a position half-way between the parallel-running cabinets of Michel 'Aun and Salim al-Hoss. After the signing of the Ta'if Agreement on 22 October, Michel 'Aun dissolved Parliament, but MPs did not abide by this decision and elected René Mu'awwad as president. The confederation recognised the legitimacy of this newly elected figurehead.[116] During this period, the confederation repeated its demand for participating in decision-making. The confederation discussed the need for a wage increase with Prime Minister al-Hoss and on 1 June 1989, a wage increase was announced.

Towards the middle of 1990, the political choices of the confederation became clearer. The strife over the Ta'if Agreement between the Lebanese army under the command of General Michel 'Aun and Samir Ja'ja''s Lebanese Forces inflicted serious damage in the Christian areas of the country. The confederation condemned the conflict.[117] On 5 April, the confederation clearly declared its position in favour of the Ta'if Agreement and thus the dissolution of militias, which was a sine qua non condition for the implementation of the agreement. From that point on, the confederation was able to set and articulate two clear priorities – the cessation of the war and the need to prevent further devaluation of the Lebanese pound. It condemned 'Aun in August and made a request to work directly with Parliament and the cabinet to set out a national peace plan. The confederation called for a march heading towards the cabinet on 23 August in support of the Ta'if Agreement and human rights, and to assert its standpoint against corruption and the militias.[118] At this point, the confederation affirmed its independence from all political parties and requested representation in the cabinet.[119] However, the newly elected President Elias Hrawi intervened to cancel the demonstration scheduled for 23 August on the grounds that it would affect the recent stability and peace.

The first action of the GCWL following the Ta'if Agreement was the first post-war National Trade Unions Conference on 20 September

1990. The conference recommendations focused on[120] implementation of the Ta'if Agreement[121] and amendment of the monetary and fiscal codes, as well as the banking secrecy regulations to protect the Lebanese currency.[122] To protect wages and guard against rising living costs, proposals included implementing indexed wages, reinforcing the national price council, controlling spiralling food prices – including a bread subsidy – and removing Article 50 of the Labour Code.[123] The GCWL also advocated for public services to be strengthened, including access to government hospitals, more support for public education and provision of clean water and electricity, along with telephone and postal services.

On 24 December 1990, Omar Karami was appointed prime minister in charge of forming the first post-war cabinet. Upon the formation of the new cabinet on 8 January 1991, the GCWL revealed during a press conference three key challenges: salary-scale adjustment and the provision of social benefits; the demands of workers in independent authorities; and the urgent demands of teachers. On 14 January 1991, the GCWL addressed these demands in a letter to the minister of labour, Albert Mansour, urging him to bring up the issue of salary adjustment. In view of increasing pressure, a joint meeting was organised on 4 February 1991 between the confederation and representatives of teaching bodies in the private and public sectors, as well as Lebanese university professors. The meeting aimed to push for salary adjustment and an indexed salary scale for public employees through unified action. All participating parties issued a common declaration focusing on four points: the unity of the union movement and joint demands, unified action pushing for a salary adjustment and an indexed salary scale, GCWL support for teachers and professors in their demands and the coordination of action.[124]

On 27 March 1992, the GCWL executive bureau objected to the Government's decision to stop subsidising wheat. The confederation also threatened to take a clear stand following the decisions in June, which was the deadline for the Government to improve the exchange rate and economic growth and declare a new indexed salary scale. Prior to the deadline set by the GCWL for 9 May 1992, mass demonstrations took place, along with several acts of violence against the Government's economic policies. These demonstrations were followed by the resignation of Prime Minister Omar Karami. Later on, union leaders confessed that the GCWL did not intend to topple the Karami Government. However, the 9 May demonstrations played a significant role in his resignation. According to other sources, the confederation was subject to manipulation during this period by the political elite that wanted to oust Karami. The strong mobilisation and action of the confederation were used to bring down Karami for reasons that were more about the interests of the political elite than the workers' demands.[125]

During the same year, the new Government of Rashid al-Solh adopted a strict monetary policy and introduced additional measures to increase government revenue to curb economic deterioration. The Government attempted to collect fines on private construction that violated the building codes during the war, especially construction on public land such as the coastline. The tax on petrol was increased;[126] however, these measures were not sufficient to curtail inflation or curb the deterioration of the exchange rate of the Lebanese pound against the US dollar. The average exchange rate for the month of September 1992 was LB2,520, reaching as high as LB2,850 by mid-September. Lebanon was in the throes of a serious economic crisis.[127]

At this point, the 1992 National Trade Unions Conference repeated the same set of demands as declared during the previous 1990 conference.[128] The conference stressed the urgent need to solve the national currency problem within a period of one month, or the GCWL would increase pressure and plan action. In 1992, the confederation called for change at all levels, including fuel, bread, medication, school tuition fees, customs fees and transport. It proposed political reforms (formation of a cabinet, the cancellation of sectarianism, a new electoral law, administrative reform and strengthening of the army) and economic reforms against privatisation and in favour of national production, along with changes in the monetary policy of the central bank, and a structural solution for wages. Despite stark socio-economic conditions in the summer of 1992, the Government insisted on conducting the first post-war parliamentary elections since 1972. Following the elections – that witnessed a significant Christian boycott due to the implications of the Ta'if Agreement – most elected deputies insisted on the appointment of Rafiq Hariri as prime minister. Rafiq Hariri was a billionaire who played a key role in the Ta'if Agreement process. He was named prime minister in October 1992. The first Rafiq Hariri cabinet marked the beginning of the reconstruction period during which the labour movement entered a new phase. The political demands of the confederation have always been pragmatic, with a flexible attitude. It managed to maintain good relations with the militias, when powerful, and rallied behind the winners in 1990. The action and mobilisation of trade unions during this period should be examined while taking into account the GCWL structure. As noted in the previous chapter, the confederation's structure restricted its scope of action to a certain extent. The GCWL included federations of different political and ideological affiliations, which rendered the decision-making process highly dependent on the consensus among parties. This decision-making process, which stemmed from the

confederation's structure, explains the limited scope of the labour movement during the civil war. During the reconstruction period, the socio-
economic and political situation changed and the labour movement was
weakened and highly politicised. Studying the history of the labour movement in Lebanon highlights several developments that are of particular
significance. The trajectory of the labour movement was from the outset
formed amid the institutionalisation of sectarianism during the French
mandate and early independence years. It was also moulded amid the
ideological concerns of political parties. Since the French mandate, trade
union federations were divided between those that closely collaborated
with right-leaning political parties which represented the leading forces
at the time, and left-wing trade unions which continuously promoted
reform without overall structural change. After gaining independence, the
'Merchant Republic' continuously restricted the rights of workers and their
freedom of association in various ways. First, the Labour Code of 1947
favoured employers, excluded a large category of workers, restrained the
workers from collective action and controlled the formation and authorisation of trade unions and federations. Second, freedom of association was
further constrained by the abstention of the Lebanese Government to ratify
the ILO Freedom of Association and Protection of the Right to Organise
Convention of 1948 (Number 87). Furthermore, when the Government
authorised the establishment of the GCWL in Lebanon in 1958, only
right-wing federations were authorised, leaving a large share of the trade
unions outside the GCWL. And finally, while all five federations that had
remained outside the GCWL rallied under its umbrella in 1970, the organisational structure of the GCWL, still in place today, was designed in a way
that made it vulnerable to political intervention and marred by limited
democratic features and representation. During the civil war, the different political and sectarian affiliations of GCWL members hampered the
adoption of a unified political vision and instead took vague positions and
adopted a flexible attitude that concealed divergent demands, a difficult
decision-making process that, in turn, produced an overall paralysis. With
this moderate position, the GCWL maintained good relations with the
militias and rallied behind the winners in 1990. These 'birth defects' and
structural restrictions explain how federations in the post-war period continued to closely collaborate with political parties including the Lebanese
Forces, the Amal Movement, Hezbollah, the Baath Party and the Future
Party. The confederation of unions became a simple reflection of rising
conflicts between political parties and the feud of the political elites over
rents and benefits, which increasingly severed the confederation from who
it was supposed to represent – the workforce.

Notes

1 *Beirut al-Massa* (5 April 1971).

2 The Ottoman Empire's Law on Associations dates from 3 August 1909, while the law governing strikes was issued on 27 July 1909. The subsequent Law on Cooperative Associations came into force in February 1910 but was amended on 24 April 1912.

3 J. Couland, *Le mouvement syndical au Liban (1919–1946): Son évolution pendant le mandat français de l'occupation à l'évacuation et au Code du Travail* (Paris: Éditions Sociales, 1970).

4 E. Boueiri, *Tarikh al-Haraka al-'Ummaliyya* (Beirut: Dar al-Farabi, 1986).

5 M. Dakroub, *Jouzour al-Sindiyana al-Hamra': Hikayat Nushou' al-Hizb al-Shuyu'i al-Lubnani 1924–1931* (Beirut: Dar al-Farabi, 2007), p. 89.

6 U. Makdisi, *The Culture of Sectarianism: Community, History, and Violence in Nineteenth-Century Ottoman Lebanon* (Berkeley: University of California Press, 2000), p. 3.

7 *Ibid.*, pp. 2–6.

8 *Ibid.*, p. 6.

9 M. Amil, *Fi al-Dawla al-Ta'fiyya* (Beirut: Dar al-Farabi, 2003), pp. 190–6.

10 *Ibid.*, p. 178.

11 *Ibid.*, pp. 193–208.

12 Salloukh et al., *The Politics of Sectarianism in Postwar Lebanon*, p. 13.

13 Makdisi, *The Culture of Sectarianism*, p. 161.

14 *Ibid.*, pp. 161–2.

15 M. Amil, *Madkhal Ila Naqd al-Fikr al-Ta'ifi: al-Qadiyya al- Filastiniyya fi Idiyulujiyyat al-Burjwaziyya al-Lubnaniyya* (Beirut: Dar al-Farabi, 1989) p. 259.

16 E. Rabbath, *La Constitution Libanaise: Origines, textes et commentaires, Section des études juridiques, politiques et administratives* (Beirut: Publications de l'Université Libanaise, 1982), pp. 5–17. According to the Chible Dammous report, stakeholders were asked whether the distribution of parliamentary seats should adopt a sectarian foundation. Respondents unanimously condemned the sectarian distribution of parliamentary seats. However, according to Rabbath, these were ingrained traditions during the *Qa'imaqamiyya* (1842–60), *Mutasarrifiyya* (1861–1915) and the French mandate, which could not be 'suddenly extracted'. Consequently, despite their general denunciation of sectarian representation, 121 respondents advocated a sectarian system; with 'great repugnance', however.

17 The constitution was promulgated on 14 May 1930.

18 J. Landau, 'Elections in Lebanon', *Western Political Quarterly*, 14:1 (1961), 120–47.

19 S. Younes, 'Histoire et Structure du Mouvement Syndical au Liban' (PhD dissertation, École pratique des hautes études, 1972).

20 F. Shimali, *Naqabat al-'ummal fi Lubnan* (Beirut, 1928), pamphlet cited by Younes, 'Histoire et Structure du Mouvement Syndical au Liban', not found.

21 Couland, *Le Mouvement Syndical au Liban*.
22 Younes, 'Histoire et Structure du Mouvement Syndical au Liban'.
23 *Confédération Générale du Travail*.
24 Younes, 'Histoire et Structure du Mouvement Syndical au Liban'.
25 Shimali, *Naqabat al-'ummal fi Lubnan*.
26 Boueiri, *Tarikh al-Haraka al-'Ummaliyya*.
27 Rabbath, *La Constitution Libanaise*, pp. 517–18.
28 A. Messarra, *La Structure Sociale du Parlement Libanais (1920–1976)* (Beirut: Lebanese University, 1977), pp. 55–6.
29 G. Corm, *Le Liban contemporain: Histoire et société* (Paris: La Découverte, 2005), p. 10. The CAS estimated the resident population in Lebanon in 2004 at 3,755,030, not including the population residing in the Palestinian camps. There are more than 400,000 Palestinian refugees officially registered in Lebanon with the United Nations Relief and Works Agency for Palestine Refugees in the Near East (UNRWA).
30 Landau, 'Elections in Lebanon', p. 128.
31 N. Shehadi, 'The idea of Lebanon: Economy and state in the Cénacle Libanais 1946–54', *Papers on Lebanon*, 5 (Oxford: Centre for Lebanese Studies, 1987).
32 T. Gaspard, *A Political Economy of Lebanon, 1948–2002: The Limits of Laissez-Faire* (Leiden: Brill, 2004).
33 G. Corm, 'L'économie dans les conférences du Cénacle libanais' in *Les Années du Cénacle* (Beirut: Dar al-Nahar, 1997), pp. 577–85.
34 *Ibid.*
35 *Ibid.*
36 Gaspard, *A Political Economy of Lebanon*, pp. 64–9.
37 C. Gates, *The Merchant Republic of Lebanon: Rise of an Open Economy* (London: I. B. Tauris, 1998), p. 80.
38 Gaspard, *A Political Economy of Lebanon*, pp. 64–9.
39 Law No. 34 (1967) specifies that foreign companies cannot replace their agents or representatives without their agreement. In turn, agents can increase the price of the imported products without fear that the company will transfer representation to another agent.
40 S. Nasr, 'Backdrop to civil war: the crisis of Lebanese capitalism', *MERIP Reports*, No. 73 (1978), 5.
41 *Ibid.*, 10.
42 K. Hamdan and M. Akl, 'Al-Tughma al-Maliyya', *Al-Tariq*, August 1979.
43 Y. Sayigh, *Entrepreneurs of Lebanon: The Role of the Business Leader in a Developing Economy* (Cambridge, MA: Harvard University Press, 1962), pp. 295–6.
44 Gates, *The Merchant Republic of Lebanon*.
45 *Ibid.*
46 Younes, 'Histoire et Structure du Mouvement Syndical au Liban', p. 53.
47 J. Donato, 'Lebanon and its labour legislation', *International Labour Review*, No. 65, 73–4.
48 *Ibid.*, 75.

49 *Ibid.*, 79–80.
50 Boueiri, *Tarikh al-Haraka al-'Ummaliyya*.
51 *Ibid.*
52 The French mandate established a tobacco and tunbac manufacturing monopoly on 1 March 1935. (Tobacco tunbac (*tombac* in French) is a type of tobacco rich in sugar, boiled in water, kept moist, and smoked with a shisha or water pipe.) Later that year the authorities established the Société Anonyme de Régie Co-Intéressée Libano-Syrienne des Tabacs et Tombacs. In 1952, the monopoly came under the control of the Lebanese state and the name of the company was changed to Société Anonyme de Régie Co-Intéressée Libanaise des Tabacs et Tombacs. 'The Régie Libanaise des Tabacs et Tombacs is a state-owned enterprise controlled by the Lebanese Ministry of Finance. The Régie aims to manage the plantation, manufacturing, trade and transport of tobacco, tunbac and its derivatives across the North, South and the Bekaa districts of Lebanon.' Régie Libanaise des Tabacs et Tombacs, accessed 5 February 2015, www.rltt.com.lb (accessed 23 November 2019).
53 Couland, *Le Mouvement Syndical au Liban (1919–1946)*, pp. 397–405.
54 According to Decision 539 of 1975, only workers in agricultural enterprises fall under the Labour Code. Article 7 of the Labour Code also excludes domestic workers and does not cover liberal professions as these fall under contractual provisions. Liberal professions are organised under 'professional associations', while civil servants fall under the legal provisions of Law-Decrees Nos. 112 and 113.
55 R. Lampman, 'The Lebanese Labor Code of 1946', *Labor Law Journal*, 5:7 (1954), 491.
56 Donato, 'Lebanon and its labour legislation', 89.
57 *Ibid.*
58 Lampman, 'The Lebanese Labor Code of 1946', p. 494.
59 *Ibid.*
60 Article 8 of Convention Number 87 stipulates that the Convention is only binding for members who have ratified it. However, the 1998 Declaration implies that this is no longer valid: 'Convention 87 is binding as a fact of membership in the ILO.'
61 ILO, 'Convention No. 87 Freedom of Association and Protection of the Right to Organise Convention', www.ilo.org/dyn/normlex/en/f?p=NORMLEXPUB:12100:0::NO::P12100_ILO_CODE:C087 (accessed 23 November 2019).
62 Boueiri, *Tarikh al-Haraka al-'Ummaliyya*.
63 *As-Safir* (27 May 1997).
64 A. Shami, *Tatawur al-Tabaqa al-'amila fi al-Ra'smaliyya al-Lubnaniyya al-Mu'asira* (Beirut: Dar al-Farabi, 1981).
65 Baroudi, 'Economic conflict in postwar Lebanon'.
66 Gaspard, *A Political Economy of Lebanon*, pp. 64–9.
67 *Institut international de recherche et de formation éducation et développement* (IRFED).

68 IRFED, *Besoins et Possibilités de Développement du Liban* (Beirut: Ministry of Planning, 1962).

69 G. Corm, *Politique Economique et Planification au Liban, 1953–1963* (Beirut: Imprimerie Universelle, 1964); A. Dagher, 'L'Etat et l'économie au Liban', *Les Cahiers du CERMOC*, No. 12 (1995), pp. 42–3.

70 Corm, *Le Liban Contemporain*, pp. 102–5.

71 Dagher, 'L'Etat et l'économie au Liban', pp. 42–3.

72 Between 1959 and 1966, the labour movement was still witnessing divisions and interventions from the Government as well as the ICFTU. The former directly intervened in trade union affairs by organising activities from its office in Beirut aimed at strengthening reformist ideology and containing communism. In fact, during 1961–62 a split occurred within the Federation of united unions. The president of the federation decided to join the ICFTU at the end of 1961. Unions of large sectors such as electricity, Régie, railway and harbour workers retreated from the federation because of its decision to join the ICFTU. Also, in 1964 the German Social Democrat Party embarked on organising union activities in Lebanon. The Party established an office in Beirut in 1965 in cooperation with the Frederich-Ebert-Stiftung (FES), created in 1964. The FES published a union affairs-related magazine *al-I'lam* in Beirut and organised training and education sessions, as well as conducting studies on union affairs.

73 *Al-Thaqafa* (3 September 1962).

74 *Jibhat al-Tahrir al-U'mali.*

75 Shami, *Tatawur al-Tabaqa al-'amila fi al-Ra'smaliyya al-Lubnaniyya al-Mu'asira*, p. 376.

76 In 1961, the minimum wage was increased from LBP93 to LBP125. In 1965, the minimum wage rose to LBP145.

77 A. Mansour, *Les Syndicats Libanais* (Beirut: Lebanese University, 1967); Consultation and Research Institute, *Al-Haraka al-Naqabiyya al-'Ummaliyya fi Lubnan* (Beirut: Arab Labour Organization, 1986).

78 Protests against the liquidation of the Palestinian resistance in Beirut followed by the Cairo agreement in 1969.

79 Other demands included national defence against Israel, wage increases, implementation of a tax law, amendment and implementation of the law pertaining to the NSSF branches, freedom of association for agricultural and other categories of workers, and defence of freedom of association.

80 Boueiri, *Tarikh al-Haraka al-'Ummaliyya.*

81 Mansour, *Les Syndicats Libanais.*

82 Younes, 'Histoire et Structure du Mouvement Syndical au Liban'. In 1960, total wage earners amounted to 125,620 and the number of unionised workers stood at 25,889. In 1965, total wage earners amounted to 149,135 and the number of unionised workers stood at 33,380.

83 Consultation and Research Institute, *Al-Haraka al-Naqabiyya al-'Ummaliyya fi Lubnan.*

84 Textile workers and employees (10.8 per cent), Tobacco Régie workers and employees (6.25 per cent) and railway workers and employees (3.45 per cent).

85 Younes, 'Histoire et Structure du Mouvement Syndical au Liban'.
86 Shami, *Tatawur al-Tabaqa al-'amila fi al-Ra'smaliyya al-Lubnaniyya al-Mu'asira.*
87 Bu Habib (2014), interviewed by Lea Bou Khater, 5 August. Bu Habib is former general secretary of the print workers' union, a labour union activist, former director of the Lebanese Trade Unions Training Centre and editor of the *Lebanese Monitor for Worker and Employee Rights.*
88 An active person, as defined by the ILO, is a person of working age who is either employed or unemployed. The activity rate is the ratio of the number of people in the labour force (employed or unemployed) to the total population.
89 F. Traboulsi, *A History of Modern Lebanon* (London: Pluto, 2007).
90 Youssef al-'Attar and Fatima Khawaja died during the demonstration and strike of Ghandour workers on 11 November 1972.
91 Hassan Hayek and Na'im Darwish were killed. Their deaths were followed by several demonstrations and general strikes.
92 D. Kallas, 'Al-Qada' yu'addi dawr fi himayat al-hurriyyat al-naqabiyya raghma al-thugurat al-kanuniyya: fahal yastajib al-musharri'', *Legal Agenda* (2 November 2012).
93 Gaspard, *A Political Economy of Lebanon*, p. 189.
94 *Ibid.*, pp. 190–2.
95 GCWL, 'Mawqaf al-Ittihad min al-wad' al-hali' (3 April 1983).
96 R. abi Habib, 'L'action de la confédération générale des travailleurs libanais (CGTL) de 1975 à 1992: portée et limites', *Annales de Sociologie et d'Anthropologie* No. 6–7 (1997), pp. 77–109.
97 *An-Nahar* (13 April 1977), p. 10.
98 *An-Nahar* (1 October 1981), p. 11.
99 *An-Nahar* (30 April 1982), p. 10.
100 *Ibid.*
101 *An-Nahar* (2 November 1985), p. 9.
102 Abi Habib, 'L'action de la confédération générale des travailleurs libanais (CGTL) de 1975 à 1992'.
103 *Al-Anwar* (23 August 1984), p. 5.
104 E. Haber, *Tawthiq Masirat al-Haraka al-Naqabiyya al-'Ummaliyya fi Lubnan 1942–1998* (Beirut: Dar al-Rihani, 2002), p. 321.
105 *Ibid.*
106 *Ibid.*
107 *Ibid.*
108 *Ibid.*
109 Bu Habib (2014), interview; Slaybi (2014), interview.
110 Antoine Bishara was president of the Federation of unions of workers in independent authorities and public and private institutions, one of the largest federations. He was the GCWL president for ten years (1983–93).
111 *An-Nahar* (1 July 1986), p. 11.
112 Haber, *Tawthiq Masirat al-Haraka al-Naqabiyya al-'Ummaliyya fi Lubnan 1942–1998.*

113 *An-Nahar* (10 July 1986), p. 9.
114 *An-Nahar* (25 October 1986), p. 9; *An-Nahar* (7 November 1986), p. 11.
115 Abi Habib, 'L'action de la confédération générale des travailleurs libanais (CGTL) de 1975 à 1992'.
116 *An-Nahar* (10 November 1989), p. 12.
117 *An-Nahar* (21 February 1990), p. 10.
118 *An-Nahar* (28 August 1990), p. 10.
119 *An-Nahar* (20 December 1990), p. 13.
120 GCWL, '"Al-Mu'tamar al-rabi": Muqarrarat wa tawsiyat al-mu'tamar al-rabi'' (20 September 1990).
121 This included the liberation of occupied territories in South Lebanon and West Bekaa and support to the displaced population guaranteeing their return to their initial place of residence.
122 Recommendations for government monetary policy also included state control over public institutions and the enforcement of state tax collection.
123 Further support for women and full benefits from the NSSF also featured in the recommendations.
124 Wage indexation is the linking of wages to an index representing the cost of living so that they are automatically adjusted up or down as that rises or falls. This particular type of indexation is called a cost-of-living increase.
125 Abi Habib, 'L'action de la confédération générale des travailleurs libanais (CGTL) de 1975 à 1992'.
126 *An-Nahar* (15 July 1992), p. 11.
127 Lebanese Central Bank, *Annual Report for 1994* (Beirut: Lebanese Central Bank, 1995).
128 GCWL, 'Qararat wa tawsiyat mu'tamar al-naqabi al-watani al-'am 1992 fi dawratihi al-khamisa' (5 June 1992).

2

Capture and control of the labour movement

This chapter examines labour relations from 1992 – the year billed as the start of the reconstruction period – until the last wage rise in 2012. This salary increase poignantly exemplifies the total co-optation and breakdown of the labour movement. The reconstruction period witnessed an active movement between 1992 and 1997, followed by fragmentation and total deactivation from the early 2000s. How and why did the labour movement fall apart, and what were the implications for Lebanon's sectarian-liberal model?

The labour movement's type of demands and actions during the post-war period was largely a continuation of the existing state of affairs before and during the war. What is often perceived as a decrease after the civil war was merely exacerbated by state intervention and co-optation, the influence of political parties and the effects of liberal economic policies, which had already been in place since independence. The result was a divided movement, and an overall cautious and moderate attitude and actions towards the Government. The times of a supposed labour movement revival, such as the 1992–97 period, were mostly fuelled by feuds among members of the elite – one section of the ruling class managing to manipulate the GCWL to fight another of Lebanon's elite groups. In addition to the long-lasting characteristics of labour relations, the post-war period witnessed intervention on a larger scale by this 'elite-cartel'[1] created by the sectarian power-sharing system, which aimed to fully co-opt the labour movement. Breaking labour power was essential to maintain this set-up and to curb opposition and change. As Hannes Baumann observes, 'the politicisation of sectarianism requires the depoliticisation of alternative social cleavages along socio-economic lines through a reframing along confessional lines. Trade union demands based on socio-economic grounds rather than sect therefore disturb the system. They provide an alternative vision of politics.'[2] Beyond controlling the labour movement to avoid a challenge to the system, the post-war period was characterised by political forces using the GCWL as an instrument in their disputes over power, rents and benefits. Under the guise of preserving confessional balances, the post-war ruling elite of businessmen and financiers organised the state incorporation of the labour movement in order to guarantee the absence of opposition and a political alternative to the sectarian-liberal system in place. And secondly, to command the hollowed-out state and secure their share of the main economic resources. This guaranteed the sustainability of Lebanon's power-sharing arrangement and the distribution of rents and benefits among the elite-cartel.

The post-war entrenchment of the sectarian-liberal forces

At the end of the civil war, most of the articles in the 1926 constitution, which institutionalised sectarianism, survived the conflict and remained in force. Hostilities in the civil war officially ended in 1990. Negotiated in Saudi Arabia in September 1989 and enacted by Parliament in November the same year, the Ta'if Agreement's amendments of the constitution retained and reinforced sectarianisation. After fifteen years of civil war, the Ta'if Agreement halted the fighting but did not lessen the presence and threat of sectarianism. As Makdisi declared, 'the war in Lebanon is now over. Sectarianism is not.'[3]

The contradictions within the Ta'if Agreement were preserved in the amendments to Article 95. It stipulated the establishment of a committee in charge of proposing measures to eliminate sectarianism, to be endorsed by the cabinet and Parliament. Conversely, at the same time, various steps were taken to reinforce sectarianism. First, the committee entrusted to abolish sectarianism was to be headed by the president of the republic and to include both the prime minister and president of Parliament. In other words, figures representing the sectarian system were put in charge of abolishing it, and the committee was never created. Secondly, the same Article 95 specified that grade-one civil servants should still be equally distributed among Christians and Muslims, which contradicted the overall aim of amending Article 95. Thirdly, in direct opposition to abolishing sectarianism, Article 22 was amended to create a sectarian-based senate to represent all 'spiritual families', which could include the participation of religious leaders.[4] Largely, the Ta'if Agreement only modified the sectarian distribution of political power and dispersed it among the president of the republic (a Christian Maronite), the president of the Council of Ministers or prime minister (a Muslim Sunni) and the president of Parliament (a Muslim Shiite). The Maronite position of president was chiefly symbolic, without real power, while greater powers were granted to the prime minister (Article 64), who became the executive head of state. The position of president of Parliament was also strengthened by extending the length of a term

from one to four years (Article 44).[5] The constitutional amendments introduced by the Ta'if Agreement also included the guiding principle for the
distribution of parliamentary seats equally between Christians and Muslims
(Article 24). It also stipulated that they should be distributed proportionally
among the sectarian groups within each community. More specifically,
since independence the parliamentary electoral system has remained a tool
to institutionalise sectarianism and strengthen the sense of sectarian identity
and solidarity. Lebanon has maintained the practice of voting, in parliamentary and municipal elections, according to district of registration rather
than place of residence. Such a practice kept people strictly affiliated to their
place of birth, even when someone had lived in another district for decades.
In other words, voting based on place of registration exacerbated the
entrenchment of traditional familial and sectarian relations and prevented
the integration of citizens in communities at their places of residence.
Radical reforms of the Lebanese electoral system have been suspended and
the continuous changes to the electoral law are considered to be superficial
cosmetic alterations. The minor scale-change mechanism is a clear indication of the fixed denominational sectarian feature of the system. Parliament
has been constantly renewed but rarely overhauled.[6] So-called Lebanese
democracy is not democracy in the real sense of the term. Its core principles,
organisation and function are based on sectarian and institutionalised discrimination. It is therefore a democracy of sectarian composition, where
subjects are not citizens but rather communities. This distorted form of
democracy can only lead to inequalities. The sectarian allocation of major
seats in governmental institutions was also mirrored in the allocation of
seats in the GCWL. In fact, since its creation in 1968 the leadership of the
confederation has always been Christian, rather than being based on any
legal provisions.[7] In 1983, when Antoine Bishara won the elections as the
LF candidate,[8] newspapers published the elected board's religious and
political affiliations alongside their names.[9] This sectarian distribution of
the board continued after the war with a change only at the level of vice-
president, which became a position held by Shiite Muslims from 2000.[10]
This amendment took into account the new balance of power installed after
the Ta'if Agreement. The sectarian restriction of the GCWL presidency is a
clear sign of the labour movement's absorption into the sectarian political
system. This explains the overall reformist approach of the labour movement in Lebanon – the confederation never questioned or opposed any
aspect of the regime. It mostly voiced demands relating to better working
conditions without expressing the need for any fundamental political
amendments. This also has to be viewed in the context of the political deadlock that characterised most of the post-war period, including a presidential
vacuum, governmental crises and election deferrals. The Ta'if Agreement

allowed for the survival of sectarian political forces. Prior to the 1975 war, relations within *zu'ama* – the sectarian ruling elite – were not harmonious, and they actually failed to put a stable political order in place. After the war, the old *zu'ama*, although weakened, did not lose all their power.[11] Militia leaders and heads of political parties became ministers.[12] They had also accumulated wealth during the war and were consolidating their holdings and partnering with businessmen of the new elite to set up business enterprises.[13] In addition, new 'expat' elites emerged from the business world, mainly contractors, and successfully converted their wealth into political power. With the start of the post-war reconstruction, the Government was inflected by serious conflicts of public and private interests. It became common for the Lebanese political class to encompass wealthy businessmen who represented the interests of the business-financial elite. Indeed, this became an inherent part of the political formation of post-war Lebanon and resulted in the creation of an 'ultra-liberal' economic model, which was in the joint interest of the business-financial and ruling political elites. Many examples of deputies and ministers who would, later on, become rich are proof of the tangled economic and political arenas. In 1996, the largest share of deputies was businessmen (30 per cent). This category included entrepreneurs, bankers, traders and industrialists, followed by lawyers and doctors.[14] Furthermore, after reconstruction, the affiliations of the GCWL leadership mirrored the political alliances at the state level. The mobilisation of the GCWL was more a reflection of political tensions and conflicts between political stakeholders than a manifestation of workers' conditions and demands. The Syrian presence in Lebanon and its interference in Lebanese internal politics also played a significant role in the control and curtailment of the labour movement. The post-war period was marred by omnipresent Syrian intervention in Lebanese affairs. After the end of the war, Syrian hegemony over Lebanon, lasting until 2005, played a key role in shaping the formation of the cabinet and political decision-making. Taking into account the size of the Syrian labour force in Lebanon and the importance of labour issues for political stability and control, ministerial posts within the Ministry of Labour had primarily been assigned to political parties that were close to the Syrian regime. This regime was eager to control labour issues as a large number of Syrian nationals worked in Lebanon. Syrians had been coming to work in Lebanon since the 1960s, when the economic boom led to a large recruitment of Syrian workers. In 1972, male Syrian nationals represented 90 per cent of total construction workers in the country.[15] During the civil war (1975–90), Lebanese migration resulted in labour shortages. After the war, the planned reconstruction resulted in massive recruitment of low-skilled male Syrian workers, who mostly worked in construction and agriculture. The number of Syrian workers in the 1990s was estimated to be between 400,000[16] and 1.4 million,[17] and according to the ILO, an estimated number of 300,000 Syrian workers were living and working in Lebanon before the outbreak of the Syrian crisis.[18]

In addition to the control of labour issues concerning Syrian nationals in Lebanon, the control of the labour movement was essential to managing political stability. The fact that the establishment of federations required pre-authorisation from the Ministry of Labour, and in addition to the prevalent intervention in GCWL elections, made it possible to use the GCWL to either put pressure on or support cabinets, meant that the Ministry of Labour's interference in GCWL decisions, actions and elections was a necessary tool. According to John Chalcraft, Syrian migrant labour in Lebanon was a sensitive issue that necessitated pro-Syrian officials' control of labour issues in general and the Ministry of Labour in particular.[19]

As a matter of fact, all ministers of labour between 1992 and 2005 – the year when the Syrian army eventually withdrew from Lebanon – were directly affiliated with political parties aligned with the Syrian regime (Baath and Syrian Social Nationalist (SSNP) parties).[20] The perpetual affiliation of ministers of labour with ruling parties, mainly during the Syrian presence, allowed for a continuous interference in the labour market and labour movement, as demonstrated below. And the firmly rooted sectarian regime and Syria's occupation and intervention in Lebanese politics led to an intensification of political intervention in the labour movement so to control any opposition to the post-war power-sharing formula.

During the post-war period, monetary and fiscal policies clearly hindered the development of the productive and private sectors. Even though industry and agriculture were not traditionally strong in pre-war Lebanon, these sectors could not be substituted in terms of job creation, equal redistribution of resources or the establishment of strong pillars for a healthy economy. The political and institutional context after the war allowed the power elite to seize state institutions and block all negotiations capable of influencing adopted policies. This elite consolidated its hegemony on political reconstruction as well as monetary and fiscal policies, and through manipulation successfully redirected state resources towards the banking sector and private interests. The seizure of the central bank, Ministry of Finance and the Council for Development and Reconstruction (CDR), among other institutions, by the political-business elite hampered all negotiations concerning the objectives and priorities between the elite and the state.[21] There was a significant overlap between private and public interests and the strong links between the elite and the banking sector. Prior to 1975, financial performance was strong and the minimalist state focused on continuing the laissez-faire strategy. From the 1990s, banks became the major beneficiaries of state economic policies. The capital of commercial banks increased to US$3.3 billion at the end of 2002, in comparison to only US$143 million in 1992.[22] This drastic increase was entirely financed by the subscription to treasury bonds. According to Addison and colleagues, the hegemony of the financial sector was common to post-war countries due to the weakening of the state institutions following the conflict.[23] In this context, economic policies did not take into account the need for national development and the public good. The political-business elite was only interested in the services and trade sector and did not develop or support the industrial and agricultural sectors. The tertiary sector was prioritised as it was considered to have a natural comparative advantage.[24] It was in this context that monetary and fiscal policies were manipulated in favour of the banking and financial sectors, leading to a rapid accumulation of public debt, a debt that was rapidly increasing due to the funding of reconstruction. While the target annual growth rate of the reconstruction programme, Horizon 2000, was around 8 per cent, the actual average rate for the 1993–2010 period only reached around 4.5 per cent, with major variations during different periods.[25] It should be noted that the post-war annual growth rate was below the 6 per cent growth-rate average registered before the war, especially during the 1960s and the first half of the 1970s.[26] The fiscal deficit remained high and public debt was rapidly increasing. In 2001, Lebanese commercial banks had for the first time more claims on the public sector than the private sector. Consequently, the private sector suffered from the crowding out of private investments by the Government's increasing demand for domestic credit. The fact that the Government paid high interest rates on treasury bonds led the banks to increase interest rates on deposits in order to secure necessary funds and to charge high interest rates on private-sector credits. Therefore, the increased government borrowing from Lebanese commercial banks led to levels of interest rates that private businesses could not afford. According to Gaspard, 'the mechanisms used have been fiscal spending and the interest and exchange rate policies. Still, the point of the argument is not about excessive spending or corruption as such, condemnable as they ought to be. Rather, it is about laissez-faire being the context or environment in which Government policy essentially operates in support of the dominant economic force, the merchant class prior to 1975, banks since 1992, and the political elite always.'[27] The result was soaring national debt. In 2006, the Lebanese debt reached more than 180 per cent of GDP – one of the highest ratios in the world. The post-war reconstruction policies had severe repercussions for the private sector in terms of productivity and employment. In 1999, the indebtedness of the state largely surpassed the borrowing of the private sector. In fact, 36 per cent of the banks' total credit (the equivalent of 90 per cent of GDP) was assigned to the Government to cover the state deficit. This deficit, which maintained high interest and borrowing rates, hampered access to credit for the private sector on the whole, but in particular for productive-sector companies. From 1999, there was a progressive decline of loans to the private sector – dropping from 34 per cent to a mere 23 per cent. Loans to the public sector increased at a faster pace compared to the private sector.[28] In addition, around 65 per cent of all loans to the private sector in 1999 were dedicated to the areas of construction and trade, while industry was only allocated 10 per cent of all loans and agriculture around 2 per cent. During this period, many industrialists and traders expressed their frustration with the crowding-out effects – the industrial sector was only able to operate at 30–50 per cent of its capacity. The high interest rates on loans were one of the main complaints that the Association of Lebanese Industrialists (ALI) and the Beirut Traders Association levelled at the post-war Government during the 1990s.[29] The effect of crowding out on the private sector and the economic recession at the end of the 1990s also had a negative impact on employment and social inequalities. While the post-war Government did increase GDP by 250 per cent between 1992 and 1998 and reconstructed Beirut's Central District, there was no economic will or vision to distribute the benefits in an equal way. This is reflected in social and economic indicators that testify to a society with increasing inequalities. As a result of the crowding-out effect, the Lebanese economy was held back and reduced to only small-sized and relatively few industrial enterprises. The total number of businesses in 2004 was 176,279, and about 90 per cent of these employed less than five workers. Just under 1,000 businesses employed more than 50 staff – translating to 0.5 per cent of the total number of Lebanese companies.[30] More significantly, 69 per cent of workers employed in the 176,279 businesses surveyed worked in what can be termed micro-businesses. This predominance of micro- and small-scale businesses is one of the key factors behind the long-standing predominance of low numbers of unionised workers in Lebanon. Moreover, a large share of the population simply remained outside the workforce and therefore outside the labour movement. In 2009, the activity rate – the rate of the total labour force to the population of working age – stood at 49 per cent, while in 1970, the activity rate for Lebanon was as low as 45 per cent.[31] When taking a closer look, this low activity rate exposes a persistently low activity rate for women (26 per cent) compared to men (73 per cent) during the same year. In addition, the labour supply in Lebanon was not only directed towards the domestic market but also targeted surrounding countries, including the Gulf nations, as well as other migration destinations. A 2009 study estimated that 45 per cent of Lebanese households had at least one migrant family member during the period 1992–2007. The migration rate for the same period was 10.3 per cent, with youth making up the largest group of migrants.[32] What is more, around 20 per cent of workers in 2010 were informal wage earners: these workers do not have access to social insurance and do not fall within the provisions of the Labour Code. Also, 36 per cent of workers were self-employed, the majority being low-skilled, performing low-production activities and having limited access to insurance schemes.[33] Informal jobs involve job insecurity and small enterprises entail a scattered workforce – both underlining the difficulties and obstacles to unionisation. The outcome is evident – Lebanon's informal economy has few unionised workers and wage earners. The number of foreign workers in 2010 was estimated at 477,000 labourers (including 90,000 Palestinian workers residing inside and outside camps), 160,000 Syrian workers and 170,000 domestic workers. In Lebanon, foreign workers cannot fully take part in union activity. Foreign workers can join existing trade unions in certain instances but cannot participate in trade union elections. As a result, they largely remain outside the workers' movement.

A vigorous labour movement, 1993–97

During the war, political demands were characterised by a moderate and tentative tone. In general, the confederation never questioned the political and economic status quo. The declaration and memorandums of the confederation give the impression that it did not often condemn the political elite nor their practices. In some instances, the memorandums accused the state, and not the political elite per se, of being indifferent to the suffering of the people. The divergence in political affiliations between the members of the confederation did not allow for a unified political stance and neutralised the confederation. The GCWL's excess precaution led to increasingly more abstract and vague political positions – leaving the confederation without bark or bite. In the post-war period, the demands of the labour movement were limited to the improvement of working and living conditions and mainly revolved around salary adjustment, expansion of workers' fringe benefits, consumer prices and rent-regulation controls. These demands did not usually go beyond seeking to improve workers' conditions to push for fundamental reforms. For instance, the GCWL's main demand focused on wage increases and demands were made regularly. These were followed by calls for strikes and demonstrations until the Government responded to the demands. Wage increases was called for almost every year, based on studies and figures published by the GCWL. However, Law No. 36 dated 16 May 1967 stipulated that the Government of Lebanon must publish a yearly cost-of-living index through the Price Index Committee (PIC). The

GCWL did not focus its demands and actions on pushing the committee to act according to the law to secure an automatic yearly indexed wage. Instead, it repeated its calls for wage increases outside the institutional mechanism already in place. The GCWL's demands were also stagnant and never progressed beyond a handful of standard demands, including an increase in salaries, fringe benefits and price and rent controls. This set of regular demands can be traced back to the early years of the GCWL and continued during the post-war period until the present day.[34] The sole exception was during Elias abu Rizq's term as president of the GCWL, when strong opposition to the state and the ruling elite was expressed. During abu Rizq's first term (1993–97), the GCWL was exceptionally active. There were several reasons for this: the election of confrontational unionist leaders, the severe deterioration of living conditions at the end of the war, and the repressive policy of the Hariri cabinets against any trade union action that would jeopardise the economic reform programme designed to aid reconstruction. However, the GCWL's performance during this period and the positions voiced by Elias abu Rizq also reflected the political alliances at state level. More precisely, Elias abu Rizq had close relations with the political opposition to Rafiq Hariri – specifically the Commander-in-Chief and later President Émile Lahhud – which shaped the positions and performance of the GCWL. During abu Rizq's presidency of the GCWL, a number of key events took place. Post-war Lebanon was marked by the prominence of Rafiq al-Hariri. He was prime minister from 1992 to 2004 apart from the two years between 1998 and 2000. Hariri became the prime minister with the longest tenure in Lebanon, and during most of this time he occupied both the position of prime minister and minister of finance.[35] Following the parliamentary elections of 1992, 20 of the 30 members of Hariri's first cabinet were newcomers to the political scene. So Rafiq al-Hariri called on his own team to step in. The central bank was now presided over by Riyad Salame, who used to be in charge of Hariri's portfolio at Merrill Lynch. Fu'ad al-Sanyura, previously employed at Citibank and who held several assignments within Hariri's enterprises, including Director of Group Méditerranée, became minister of finance.[36] In 1991 al-Fadel Shalaq, the previous director of OGER[37] and the Hariri Foundation, stepped into the role of president of the CDR. Similarly, Suhayl Yammut, previously in charge of Hariri's business in Brazil, became the governor of Mount Lebanon. Michel Makari, vice-president of the Hariri-owned Saudi OGER, took up the post of minister of telecommunications.[38] Shortly after Rafiq Hariri came to power in October 1992, in 1993 the CDR presented to Parliament a reconstruction strategy entitled 'Horizon 2000 for Reconstruction and Development', with a budget of US$14.3 billion to be spent over a period of ten years between 1993 and 2002. The plan was subject to fierce criticism by economists, architects and various stakeholders. One of the most criticised aspects of Horizon 2000 was that it overlooked the problems of poverty and economic inequality and only focused on infrastructure and construction. Importantly, Parliament had passed Law No. 117 two years earlier, amending the Law-Decree concerning the establishment of the CDR and permitting the reconstruction of Beirut's central district to be assigned to a single real-estate company – namely, Solidere.[39] This law was immediately considered to be anti-constitutional and against the 'rights of the people'. Solidere affected around 120,000 individuals, owners and tenants, whose property rights were transformed into financial rights within the company as they became shareholders.[40] As soon as Hariri became prime minister, the GCWL presented a list of demands comprising wage increases, workers' benefits, price regulations, rent controls, independence of the labour-movement guarantees and participation in the design of the post-war reconstruction plans. The Government did not respond to the demands and the GCWL President Antoine Bishara expressed disappointment at the Hariri cabinet's disregard; in particular, the neglect of education, healthcare and social safety nets for workers and other vulnerable groups.[41] Shortly afterwards, on 8 July 1993, the GCWL organised executive council elections and surprisingly, the coalition headed up by Antoine Bishara and backed by the Government lost. Bishara had made a deal with the minister of labour and removed candidates with strong leftist affiliations from his lists. In return, Minister of Labour Abdallah al-Amin backed his candidacy as president in an attempt to prevent the election of anti-government candidates.[42] During every GCWL election in the post-war period, the Government intervened in one way or another. In 1993, it sided with the coalition headed by Antoine Bishara running against Elias abu Rizq. Since then, the Ministry of Labour has intervened in every executive council election by requiring the submission of the electoral roll and list of candidates before elections. Legal provisions regulating trade unions did not stipulate this practice. Failure by the GCWL to submit these election details was usually followed by the Ministry of Labour's refusal to validate the election results. For instance, the Ministry refused to validate the elections in 1997. The intervention and meddling in the electoral process succeeded in securing the necessary votes for pro-government candidates but also caused a split within the confederation in both 1997 and 1999. Bishara lost the support of left-wing and communist delegates, because of his deal with the Government. Many delegates voted for the opponent's list, headed by Elias abu Rizq in response to Bishara's weak reaction to the Government's interference. Elias abu Rizq was an employee of the national television network Télé Liban. He was elected president of the Union of workers and employees of Télé Liban and was later voted in as president of the Federation of united trade unions. Most of the independent and left-wing candidates won in the elections and Elias abu Rizq was elected president. Out of 44 votes, abu Rizq received 23, as against 21 for Bishara.[43] Six months later, the GCWL executive council filed a lawsuit against Bishara, accusing him of not completing the handover of his executive bureau's administrative and financial matters.[44]

With the election of the new executive council in July 1993, a new cycle of labour relations began, where the confederation was both active and vocal. Labour relations witnessed a series of confrontations between the successive Hariri cabinets and the GCWL, which also reflected conflicts between the prime minister and his opponents. Three factors explain the surge of workers' action and pressure during the 1993–97 period. First, the GCWL elected two assertive and confrontational leaders in July 1993 to head up the executive board – Elias abu Rizq as president and Yasir Ni'ma in the post of secretary-general.[45] Elias abu Rizq was backed by leftist political parties. Yasir Ni'ma had left-wing political affiliations as a founding member of the Organisation of Lebanese Socialists in 1968 and the Communist Action Organisation in 1972. He worked as both a journalist and as the general director of the leading Lebanese newspaper *as-Safir* in 1984. He was also the president of the trade union of employees of newspapers, magazines and news agencies in Lebanon. Second, the militancy of the two leaders implied the extension of their demands and positions within the political realm, which caused an aggressive reaction from the Government. Elias abu Rizq was supported by several MPs who were against Prime Minister Rafiq Hariri, mainly Najah Wakim, Zahir al-Khatib and Habib Sadiq, as well as Hezbollah, the Phalanges Party, former Prime Ministers Omar Karami and Salim al-Hoss and Deputy Nassib Lahhud.[46] Abu Rizq also had good connections with the Lebanese Army's Commander-in-Chief and later President of the Republic, Émile Lahhud, who was also hostile to Hariri. It is this polarisation of political parties and forces which to a large extent defined the demands and actions of the GCWL during this period. Abu Rizq launched a campaign against the political and economic policies of all Hariri cabinets, starting with his first GCWL leadership period in 1993. The GCWL became a key player in the political opposition to Rafiq Hariri.

Third, living conditions in Lebanon deteriorated enormously at the end of the civil war, as previously explained. These difficult conditions generated increased mobilisation fuelled by a reconstruction strategy that overlooked social and development objectives. After the elections of its new executive board in summer 1993, the GCWL entered into dialogue with Minister of Labour Abdallah al-Amin, discussing a list of demands. In November 1993, the Ministry of Labour and the GCWL reached an agreement on wage increases, benefits and price controls. Subsequently, the Government failed to respect the agreement.[47] The following year, the GCWL reiterated its demands several times. In September 1994, it submitted a detailed declaration to the president, the Council of Ministers and Parliament presenting the demands for wage increases, workers' benefits and regulations on rent control and consumer prices. In December 1994, the same package of demands was presented at the sixth session of the National Trade Unions Conference.[48] The confrontation between the GCWL and the Hariri cabinet continued throughout 1995 – as soon as Hariri was appointed to head his second cabinet on 25 May 1995. Political forces resorted to the old tried-and-tested tactics of divide and rule. The prime minister and the minister of labour aimed to weaken the labour movement mainly through the division of its leadership. They encouraged the former President of the GCWL Antoine Bishara to distance himself from Elias abu Rizq by suspending the membership of the federation over which he presided, the Federation of independent authorities, from the confederation's executive council. In support of Bishara, the federations of trade unions of bank employees and workers and employees of airline companies both suspended their membership of the executive board.[49] Bishara revived a sectorial federation that had been licensed in 1970 – the Federation of sectorial trade unions – and grouped under it 6 of GCWL's 22 member federations. According to Bishara, the rebirth of the federation aimed to provide a legal body grouping together the leadership that was opposed to the policies of abu Rizq.[50] In February the following year, the GCWL expressed its opposition to the economic and political policies of the Government at the seventh session of the National General Conference of Trade Unions. It comprised a fervent accusation of the Government for its poor economic policies, public debt, trade and budgetary deficits, high interest rates and the deterioration of workers' living conditions. It set a one-month ultimatum for the Government to address the list of demands before calling for a general strike and mass demonstrations.[51] In addition to the economic critique, the conference report also tackled political issues. The report criticised the new Press Law and the ban on demonstrations as a serious violation of freedom and rights. Unlike his predecessors, who were reticent to address political matters, abu Rizq several times stated the need to respect Lebanese citizens' basic political rights. Political demands were predominantly voiced under his leadership. He was a key opponent of and actively campaigned against the Press Law of 1962 that restricted political freedom, and the ban on television and radio stations, including drafting a GCWL action plan concerning freedom. During this period, the prime minister rejected any negotiations with the GCWL on political issues such as the Press Law and the right of the Government to ban all demonstrations – in effect demarcating clear limits to the GCWL's remit. Following this episode, Hariri and abu Rizq actually met to discuss the previous events, as Hariri appeared to be willing to take into account some of the criticisms directed at his economic programme.[52] At this meeting at the prime minister's residence, abu Rizq reiterated the confederation's demands. In March 1996, business leaders revealed they were ready to discuss labour demands and wage increases. Consequently, the PIC[53] held a set of meetings in March 1996 to identify the increases in the price of basic goods and services during 1995 and to determine the cost-of-living adjustment that should be carried out for 1996.[54] While the GCWL demanded a 76 per cent wage increase, business representatives were unwilling to offer more than 15 per cent. At this point, the committee suspended its meetings.[55] As a response to the Government's silence and inaction, the GCWL decided to use the imminent visit of the French President Jacques Chirac to pressure the Government and therefore issued an ultimatum: the Government would answer the workers' demands immediately or the workers would organise a sit-in outside Parliament coinciding with President Chirac's speech on 6 April 1996.[56] Throughout that day, the Lebanese army blocked the entrance to the GCWL's headquarters and prevented those inside from marching to Parliament.[57] Instead, the sit-in was held inside the headquarters and was covered by the media. In April 1996, Israel launched 'Operation Grapes of Wrath' against Lebanon and conducted extensive shelling for 16 days in what it claimed was an attempt to stop Hezbollah's rocket attacks. Following the April war, in May 1996, the Government approved a scheme for wage increases and other benefits for private-sector workers. On one side of the wage dispute, business associations rejected the scheme, arguing that it would lead to financial burdens. On the other, the GCWL also rejected the proposal as it fell way below the requested 76 per cent increase. Right after the parliamentary elections on 25 September 1996, Elias abu Rizq attacked the Government again. During a political gathering of leaders opposing the Hariri cabinet, abu Rizq launched a strong critique of the Government's plans to close almost all private television and radio stations.[58] He also restated all GCWL's demands on behalf of workers and declared the confederation's readiness to call for strikes and mass demonstrations against the Government's violation of the freedom of speech and the media.[59] Despite the government ban, abu Rizq called for a sit-in opposite government headquarters a few days later on 4 October and a general strike to be staged on 10 October in tandem with a mass demonstration. As usual, the army intervened to prevent the scheduled sit-in and banned the demonstrations. Following every parliamentary election, a new government is formed. On 7 November Hariri formed his third cabinet, and on 28 November 1996, the GCWL again attempted to organise demonstrations against the media ban and the poor economic and social conditions. Unsurprisingly, the demonstrations were violently thwarted by the army.

Cracking the GCWL: 1997 executive elections

State repression of the labour movement through legal and structural manipulation took a new turn at the 1997 GCWL elections. The state's meddling in the elections aimed to oust the president of the GCWL and thus weaken its opposition to state decisions and policies. The ruling elite's interference relied on the political and sectarian affiliations of trade unionists that shaped the elections. GCWL members' voting was influenced by clear instructions given by the political parties – in Lebanon, affiliation to a political party is almost always equivalent to sectarian affiliation. In 1997, Prime Minister Rafiq Hariri and President of the Parliament Nabih Birri decided to attack the GCWL leadership. Relations between Hariri and abu Rizq had already been tense for some time, but a conflict between different political players produced and shaped the strike against abu Rizq. The confrontation between Hariri and abu Rizq reflected a conflict in the balance of power within the post-war sectarian political system, rather than a conflict between workers, trade unions and the state. As mentioned earlier, abu Rizq had close relations with the political opposition to Hariri, mainly with the Commander-in-Chief Émile Lahhud – another of Hariri's political opponents. At the beginning of 1997, Hariri attempted to halt the promotion of six colonels, including Jamil al-Sayyid, who had a close relationship with the Syrian regime, and Lahhud. Following Syrian pressure, Hariri was forced to allow the promotions. The 1997 GCWL elections presented an opportunity for Hariri to counter the increasing power of Lahhud by campaigning against the election of abu Rizq. Hariri rallied Lahhud's opponents, including Nabih Birri and As'ad Hirdan, and also trade union leaders who had previously clashed with abu Rizq, such as Antoine Bishara. Birri and abu Rizq were also political rivals. In the 1996 parliamentary elections, As'ad Hirdan, who was on Nabih Birri's list, ran against Elias abu Rizq for the Orthodox Christian seat in the Hasbaya-Marja'yun electoral area. The following year Birri and abu Rizq clashed again when the GCWL executive council opposed the admission of five new federations that were politically affiliated to the Amal Movement headed by Birri.[60] At the beginning of 1997, Minister of Labour As'ad Hirdan launched a campaign against abu Rizq to topple him at the 1997 GCWL elections. The affiliation of the ministers of labour with the ruling parties made it possible to pressure the GCWL when necessary, as the Ministry of Labour controlled the budget allocated to the GCWL. During the presidential terms of Elias abu Rizq, the Ministry of Labour's budget allocation to the GCWL – amounting to LBP 500 million (US$333,000) – was withheld in 1996 and only released after the departure of abu Rizq in 2000. Hence, it was a key strategic tool to influence and weaken the GCWL, because the annual funding from the Ministry of Labour is its only regular source of finance, as member federations generally do not pay any membership fees.[61] During this period, the Government was accused of intervening in the elections of several federations in order to guarantee pro-government representatives on the GCWL executive council. This was intended to guarantee a majority of votes cast against abu Rizq. For instance, on 13 April 1997, the elections of the Federation of the workers of South Lebanon were subject to widely documented government interference.[62] Newspapers reported on the rigged elections and critics warned against similar government intervention in the upcoming GCWL elections.[63] The result was five pro-government delegates on the executive council who were guaranteed to vote against the re-election of abu Rizq.

Only a few days before the GCWL elections, the Ministry of Labour also authorised the creation of five new federations, despite being rejected by the GCWL during the previous four years.[64] The authorisations secured ten additional pro-government delegates on the executive council.[65] The federations had not been rejected, but new federations required two-thirds of the votes of the executive council and CR according to the regulations of the confederation. If rejected, a federation wanting to join could resort to the judiciary. The Ministry of Labour was not entitled to impose the admittance of federations on the confederation. According to the Minister of Labour, the ministry relied on Articles 93 and 94 of the Labour Code,[66] in addition to two judiciary consultations.[67] The five federations applied for membership to the GCWL four years prior to the April 1997 elections, but the Ministry of Labour only intervened four days before election day – timing that drew attention to the role and intervention by the Government in the elections. The five newly licensed federations had clear political and sectarian affiliations to Nabih Birri's Shiite Amal Party.[68] In fact, Bassam Tlays, president of the Workers' Bureau of the Amal Movement, acted as a spokesperson for the five federations, which was a clear indication of their political allegiance. Furthermore, the federations were licensed only a few days before the elections of the GCWL executive council and yet were going to participate in the elections, even though the confederation had not accepted their membership.[69] At this point, the 22 member federations of the GCWL, plus the 5 newly authorised ones, participated in the elections on 24 April 1997.[70] Out of the 27 federations, 11 were opposed to the current GCWL leadership, including the newly admitted 5 plus the federations of bank employees, aviation employees, independent authorities, maritime workers, league of unions and food products and leisure.

On 24 April 1997, two different elections for the GCWL executive bureau took place, and several irregularities were witnessed. The first election was held at GCWL's premises without the presence of Ministry of Labour representatives, as the ministry refused to observe the polling. Delegates from 12 federations loyal to abu Rizq re-elected him as president. Of the 26 delegates who attended these elections, 24 voted for abu Rizq.[71] Eyewitness accounts from delegates describe the elections as taking place under the heavy presence of state security officers, who prevented other delegates from entering the premises.[72]

One hour later – in the very same building – another round of elections was held, under Ministry of Labour supervision and broadcast on national TV. The five recently licensed new federations politically affiliated with Nabih Birri attended this election. According to the Ministry of Labour, 35 delegates out of 54 cast their votes in favour of 12 pro-government members, with Ghanim al-Zughbi elected as president.[73] These elections marked the first clear split in the labour movement despite having been resilient to internal division during the civil war. The division of the confederation was the result of the state's intervention and thus corruption of the elections through the manipulation of legal provisions. Unsurprisingly, the Ministry of Labour recognised the results of the second elections. The newly elected leadership paid a protocol visit to the President of the Republic Elias Hrawi, Prime Minister Rafiq Hariri and President of the Parliament Nabih Birri.[74] Abu Rizq also claimed the presidency – abu Rizq declared his own victory while internal security forces halted media coverage. He was soon supported by political figures, notably government opponents, including former Prime Minister Salim al-Hoss.[75] MP Mustafa Sa'ad, Hezbollah, the LCP and the Communist Action Organisation all published a communiqué in support of abu Rizq's election win and denouncing the intervention of the Government.[76] This was followed by the support of ILO representatives and the International Federation of Arab Unions, together with the International Federation of Free Unions in Brussels, which also condemned the electoral process.[77] Hassan Jammam, the representative of the International Federation of Arab Unions, said: 'What happened during these elections aims to destroy the labour movement and I have never seen such interference during my 25 years of union practice.' And Georges Martinez, director of the legal department at the International Federation of Free Trade Unions, stated: 'I just witnessed the worst aggression against democracy and union freedom which has ever occurred in any democratic state.'[78] The most confrontational labour relations in the history of Lebanon took place during Elias abu Rizq's term as GCWL president.

Under his leadership, the GCWL questioned and challenged almost every policy of the three Hariri cabinets. Hariri was determined to prevent the GCWL from imposing concessions on the Government and therefore mobilised all resources against abu Rizq, including government intervention in elections with the support of the judiciary branch, which ultimately validated the victory of his rival, Ghanim al-Zughbi.[79] Nevertheless, the backcloth to the confrontation between Hariri and abu Rizq must be viewed through the lens of struggles for control and power within Lebanon's postwar sectarian-liberal system, rather than a strict conflict between workers' unions and the state. The intervention of political parties and forces has continued to intensify and thus has increasingly shaped the demands and actions of the GCWL in post-war times.

Under the newly elected leadership, the GCWL became more cooperative in its relations with the Government and business associations. The election of al-Zughbi in 1997 relaunched the dialogue between the Government, business associations and workers. However, the Government offered no concessions to the GCWL during al-Zughbi's term, which led to his resignation in 1998. His term was marked by the repetition of demands, strike suspensions and a distinct lack of achievements. Demands were repeated to no avail and when strikes were undertaken, they were only partially respected. Upon his election, al-Zughbi declared that the GCWL would demand a new salary scale and if the Government was not responsive, it would resort to strikes and demonstrations. However, he specified that the GCWL sectorial federations would only exert pressure on the Government without 'breaking down the country' and staging demonstrations. The key demands voiced during this term revolved around the enactment of a new minimum wage in both public and private sectors, activation of all tripartite committees,[80] the draft of a new labour code, and pushing through a validation of the confederation's internal regulations.[81] During his short term of office, al-Zughbi explicitly made public his will to conduct a dialogue among trade union leaders to bridge the divide in the labour movement. And he declared he would resign should he fail to achieve unity in the labour movement.[82]

Co-optation through 'hatching'

As demonstrated above, it is through the authorisation of additional federations that the Ministry of Labour succeeded in 'cracking' the GCWL. In fact, the main strategy used by the ruling elite to weaken and co-opt the labour movement during the post-war period was to grant an excessive number of authorisations to federations through the Ministry of Labour. It is, therefore, necessary to pause and examine the process of 'hatching', which refers to the creation of additional trade union federations.[83] The number of federations in the GCWL increased from a mere 22 in 1993 to 36 in 2001,[84] before reaching a staggering 59 federations in 2015.[85] Two main reasons may explain the creation of federations. First, the creation of new federations awarded additional votes within the executive council and therefore allowed them to shape GCWL decisions. Second, players outside the confederation, such as political parties, found their way in through the creation of new federations that were awarded votes in the executive council. With excessive numbers of authorisations, the structure of the confederation reflected a fragmented and scattered labour movement that did not mirror the profile and characteristics of the workforce. In general, the increasing number of federations stemmed from political and strategic decisions, mainly electoral engineering, that denoted the political structure of the country.

In principle, the GCWL includes all trade union federations under its structure. Before the outbreak of the civil war in 1975, the confederation comprised 18 federations. During the war period from 1975 to 1989, 6 new federations joined the confederation. Remarkably, the first decade in the post-war period (1990–99) witnessed the creation of 19 new federations, which account for 32 per cent of total federations today, the largest share among the different time periods. This increase took place during a period marred by political tensions between the Government and the confederation leadership. The Government responded to the opposing stands of the confederation by increasing the number of pro-government federations in a strategic move to increase its control of the decision-making of the confederation. During the tenure of Minister of Labour Abdallah al-Amin, the authorisations of new federations increased massively. This increase did not originate from, nor reflect the characteristics of the labour market and the workforce.[86] Between 2000 and 2005, 14 federations were created, meaning that 24 per cent of the total number of federations was created during this period. However, in the following ten years, between 2006 and 2016, only two new federations were approved.

The increase in federations had inflated the size of the executive council, given that all members had an equal number of votes regardless of their actual representative size. The weak organisational structure of the confederation, which was mainly marked by the lack of proportional representation, allowed for political intervention through the creation of more trade unions and federations, therefore increasing the weight of small federations in the voting process.[87] The political affiliation of these small federations could be used as a tool to block any attempt at organisational reform, mainly the reform proposed in 1996. Organisational reform that promoted proportional representation implied the shrinking power of the majority

Table 2 Distribution of federations in the GCWL by date of authorisation

Date of authorisation	Total	%
Before 1975	18	31
During the war, 1976–89	6	10
1990–99	19	32
2000–05	14	24
2006–16	2	3
Total	59	100

Source: Author's calculations, based on data collected from the Ministry of Labour.

of trade unions in the decision-making process. The lack of proportional representation distorted the representation so that the smallest federation of 200 members had the same number of votes as the largest federation of 9,000 members.[88] In other words, proportional representation would limit the political influence of parties and ruling elites. Data collected from the Ministry of Labour are based on the federations declaring their voter lists. These data show that the majority of federations were active (58 per cent), as they conducted their latest elections between 2011 and 2015. The remaining share (41 per cent) consists of dormant federations that have conducted no elections since 2010. The lack of recent elections reflects the stagnation of their action and may infer that these federations were solely authorised as part of the 'hatching' strategy.

While observing the number of federations and trade unions across periods, results underline a trend in the evolution of federations throughout the four time periods covered by this research. Before the war, a small number of federations represented a large number of trade unions. Conversely, after the war, the number of federations increased, however, comprising a smaller number of trade unions. This trend shows that the increasing number of federations after the war did not reflect a proportional

Table 3 Distribution of federations by date of last election and type

Time period	Total	%
1990–95	1	2
1996–2000	2	3
2001–05	4	7
2006–10	17	29
2011–15	34	58
N/A	1	2
Total	59	100

Source: Author's calculations, based on data collected from the Ministry of Labour.

Table 4 Distribution of trade unions by date of authorisation

Period	No.	%
Before 1975	118	36
1975–89	38	12
1990–2015	172	52
Total	328	100

Source: Author's calculations, based on data collected from the Ministry of Labour.

Table 5 Distribution of trade unions belonging to more than one federation, 2015

Federations (no.)	Trade unions (no.)
Trade unions that are members in 2 federations	59
Trade unions that are members in 3 federations	4
Trade unions that are members in 4 federations	1

Source: Author's calculations, based on data collected from the Ministry of Labour.

increase in the number of trade unions and thus did not reflect changes in the labour market. Therefore, creation of federations seems to be intertwined with the political conflict between the Government and the GCWL.

The increasing number of trade unions during this period is another indication of a fragmented and scattered labour movement. It is important to note that trade unions can belong to several federations at the same time. In 2015, sixty-four trade unions were represented in two or more federations. The strategy of multiple memberships has been criticised by several observers, who note that the creation of new federations only serves the purpose of controlling the decision-making of the GCWL.[89]

It is necessary to note that the multiplication of federations was not accompanied by an increase in unionisation; on the contrary, the share of unionised workers continued to dwindle. In 2001, there were 238 trade unions with a total of 78,829 members, but the average number of members per trade union stood at 331.[90] In 2015, the number had jumped to a total of 286 trade unions, while the post-war period, on the other hand, saw a dwindling of unionised workers.[91] The share of unionised workers in 2001 was as low as 10.6 per cent of total wage earners. However, a more conservative scenario considers only the number of active members that voted in their trade union's most recent board elections. According to this scenario, the share of unionised workers dropped to 7.7 per cent.[92] And in 2015, 5.2 per cent of surveyed wage earners were unionised. Strikingly, the share of unionised women workers was more than double the share of men: 3.2 per cent of men were members of trade unions versus 8.8 per cent of women. This is due to the predominance of women in the education sector, which has always had one of the largest trade unions. In conclusion, the higher numbers of federations in the post-war period did not reflect an increase in the number of trade unions nor changes in the labour market. The higher numbers were rather a result of the political conflict between the Government and leaders of the labour movement and the Government's attempt to control the decision-making of the GCWL. The consequence of the co-optation of the labour movement has been the absence of labour power that could effectively oppose the harsh sectarian-liberal system. The labour movement has presented no political alternative that could strengthen and maintain the demands of the October uprising in 2019, when people were fighting for change and a new political system. The 2019 October uprising was to take up the same struggle as the labour movement in the early 1990s; however, against a harsher and more entrenched system, and this time with a silenced labour movement.

Capture of the executive council

In May 1997, three federations allied with Elias abu Rizq filed a lawsuit against the GCWL, requesting that the judiciary revoke the election results endorsed by the Ministry of Labour and declare them void due to the reported irregularities and violations.[93] The Second Chamber of the Court of First Instance in Beirut issued a decision that refused the case and did not nullify the election results in favour of al-Zughbi.[94] In a counter-move, the GCWL filed a lawsuit against its former President Elias abu Rizq, accusing him of usurpation of title and civil authority.[95] Abu Rizq did assign a delegation on behalf of the GCWL to the ILO's 85th Session in Geneva. The general prosecutor of the Court of Appeal in Beirut summoned abu Rizq to a hearing in the case. On 30 May 1997, abu Rizq was interrogated for three hours, and by order of the general prosecutor, he was kept in custody at the Palace of Justice.[96] He was hospitalised over the following two days under strict security. Meanwhile, the International Global Labour Summit taking place in Copenhagen, which abu Rizq was invited to attend, addressed an official letter to the president of the republic demanding the release of abu Rizq and expressing its concern about the breach of trade union freedoms.[97] Abu Rizq was not able to attend the 85th Session of the ILO as planned, and al-Zughbi headed up the GCWL delegation. Abu Rizq's arrest triggered a series of reactions from political and trade union officials.[98] A few days later, the former GCWL Secretary-General Ni'ma was arrested in relation to the same case. Another lawsuit was filed against abu Rizq for tarnishing the image of the state by addressing two letters to the ILO, in which he referenced the occurrence of bribery during the 1997 elections. Abu Rizq was released eight days later on a LBP 400,000 (US$265) bail, while the two cases against him were still open. As soon as he left hospital, he declared that he was arrested because 'the Government feared another 6 May', referring to the events that unseated Omar Karami in 1992.[99] In July 1997, the GCWL gave the Government an ultimatum of fifteen days to take action on the demands made by the newly elected leadership in May 1997 – mainly the formation and activation of the tripartite dialogue. The Government remained inactive on that front and thus the confederation declared its support for a popular movement, dubbed the 'Hunger Revolution',[100] which was to take place in Baalbek on 5 July 1997. Abu Rizq soon issued a communiqué in support of the call for protest and civil disobedience in response to the Government's policies.[101] At the end of July, the cabinet organised a closed meeting with key economic stakeholders to elaborate on the main socio-economic recommendations. The GCWL protested that it had not been invited to participate in the discussions and asserted that the enactment of the Economic and Social Council (ESC) as specified in the Ta'if Agreement was a priority for Lebanon – not closed meetings. In November 1997, the GCWL threatened several times to call a general strike to demand a wage adjustment and a minimum monthly wage set at US$330. After a series of negotiations with the cabinet, no settlement was reached and a strike was called for 13 October. However, the strike was only partially respected, especially by employees working at state enterprises and private schools. The strike was considered a failure because coordination between the state and business associations limited its scope.[102] The political conflict between Prime Minister Rafiq Hariri and President of the Parliament Nabih Birri affected the size of the strike. Birri had managed to block an attempt by Hariri to organise municipal elections for fear of losing ground in South Lebanon to Hezbollah. Also, Birri and ministers affiliated with the Amal Movement had launched a campaign against Hariri's plans to increase taxes on fuel and car registration. As a result, institutions associated with Birri respected the strike (Tobacco Régie and the NSSF), whereas those linked to Hariri (the Port of Beirut) did not strike.[103] Another strike was planned for 25 and 26 November with a number of demands, mainly pushing for an increase of end-of-service indemnity for workers. This strike was postponed until the end of the year to allow time for negotiations between business associations and the Ministry of Labour.[104] The ability of Hariri and Birri to influence – and to a large extent control – the scope of the workers' strike underscores the importance of political and sectarian affiliations, which have tended to supersede workers' affiliation to trade unions and respect for the GCWL's decisions.

In 1998, abu Rizq started to take action under a new organisation named the Independent GCWL, which was made up of a coalition of federations supporting him. For several months, the GCWL and the Independent GCWL issued parallel actions, which exacerbated the rift in the labour movement. In January 1998, the government budget proposal included higher taxes and lower spending on infrastructure development to bring down the budget deficit. The GCWL called a sit-in outside Parliament on 22 January, which was attended by several MPs including Nayla Mu'awwad, Najah Wakim, Zahir al-Khatib, Hussein Hajj-Hassan and Ali Hussein Khalil.[105] The Independent GCWL moved its planned sit-in from 22 to 26 January. Hezbollah, LCP and SSNP officials, as well as MPs who attended the previous GCWL sit-in such as Najah Wakim and Zahir al-Khatib, also attended the independent GCWL's sit-in protest.[106] Nonetheless, Parliament approved the 1998 budget proposal with increased taxes and with no funds to introduce a new public-sector salary scale.

The GCWL repeated its series of unmet demands with a plan to escalate sit-ins, strikes and protests.[107] On 25 February, the Union of workers and employees in grain silos in Beirut organised an open-ended strike to put into practice end-of-service compensation (Decision 161/92) and to demand that daily workers should be given permanent contracts, and have fringe benefits included in their collective contract.[108] Meanwhile, the Independent GCWL demanded wage adjustments for the years 1997 and 1998, and a new taxation policy.[109] The Government did not respond to the GCWL's demands regarding the enactment and activation of a tripartite dialogue. Rather, the Ministry of Labour drafted a decree establishing the management board of the NSSF without any representatives from the GCWL – the body with the highest representation of workers in Lebanon.[110]

The Ministry of Labour continued to interfere in trade union elections, insisting that the electoral list should be submitted to the ministry prior to voting. In March 1998, the ministry halted the voting of the Federation of workers and employees of independent authorities and public institutions and requested the submission of electoral lists before polling day.[111] The elections of the CR of this federation took place two weeks later and were subject to government pressure to vote for a pro-government president. While federation members had earlier agreed to vote for Talal Hajjar, they instead elected Shawki Ismail as president of the CR.[112] The following month, the executive council chose Fu'ad Harfush (trade union of Litani workers) as president and Tariq al-Rafi'i (trade union of electricity workers) as secretary-general of the executive bureau. While the president and secretary-general of the executive bureau were supposed to represent the federation at the GCWL, other executive bureau members were picked instead because of government pressure.[113] In April 1998, al-Zughbi

resigned from the GCWL presidency in protest against the lack of government cooperation on any of the demands put forward by the GCWL. He
called for new elections to take place the following July. Elias abu Rizq
announced his candidacy for the GCWL presidency and this time abu Rizq
enjoyed the full support of his previous rival and the Amal Movement, following negotiations. To gain the support of Nabih Birri, president of Amal
and the Parliament, abu Rizq was required to acknowledge the legitimacy of
the five Amal-affiliated federations authorised by the Ministry of Labour in
1997, which had caused the rift within the GCWL. He also recognised the
legitimacy of the former GCWL executive council, to which he presented
his candidacy. He withdrew the lawsuits filed against the GCWL; however,
the GCWL continued to proceed with their legal claims. By making such
substantial concessions, abu Rizq increased the power of Birri within the
GCWL. Once again, the political rift between Birri and Hariri reflected on
the GCWL: Birri, one of the most influential representatives of the Shiite
community, now held more power within the executive council, given the
number of delegates affiliated to the Amal Movement. Abu Rizq had taken
a political side by forging an alliance with Birri against Rafiq Hariri – his
long-standing adversary.[114] The concessions made by abu Rizq explained
the substantial restrictions and co-optation characterising his second term.

On 31 July 1998, abu Rizq was elected president with 32 votes out
of 52.[115] Bassam Tlays, a member of the Amal Movement, was elected
secretary-general for Arab Affairs, with a total of 38 votes. The election
of Tlays is a clear indication of long-lasting infiltration by political parties
and of the Amal Movement's control over the GCWL resulting from the
agreement with abu Rizq prior to his election. Consequently, the Amal
Movement from that moment on would co-opt the confederation's decisions and actions for the following two decades. On 14 August, the newly
elected executive council met for the first time and issued a memorandum
focusing on a number of demands,[116] but critically did not reference the
need for amending internal regulations or a new trade union structure.
Since the 1990s, the GCWL had frequently stated the need to reform the
organisational structure of the GCWL and adopt proportional representation of federations. In January 1993, Antoine Bishara presented a new
proportional organisational design of the confederation to the Ministry
of Labour, which did not approve the plans. Proportional representation
would mean that a federation – regardless of the size of its membership –
would no longer necessarily be represented by four delegates in the CR and
two delegates in the executive council. An overhaul of the electoral system
based on proportionality would ensure that the size of a federation's membership matched the share of representatives it received. Hence, larger federations, representing more members, would be allocated more delegates in

the CR and executive council. In Lebanon, federations of public authorities, which had the most members, would have the largest number of delegates. Under his first term, Elias abu Rizq retracted the proposed reorganisation from the Ministry of Labour, as it comprised, according to abu Rizq, structural flaws that would paralyse the confederation. The GCWL looked at options to reform the union structure in Lebanon based on the experience of Arab and foreign countries. The proposal of a new union structure would allow all similar unions to group together under federations. The revised organisational design was submitted to the Ministry of Labour in 1995, which did not approve the changes.[117] Since then, the revised structure of the GCWL has been pending and is no longer an expressed demand. Taking into account the concessions of abu Rizq before his re-election in 1998, the newly elected executive council did not reiterate the necessity for a new organisational structure. An electoral reform of the GCWL based on the principle of proportionality would have lessened the extent of political interference, and thus hampered the influence of the ruling elite in general and Birri in particular. Once again, state repression was demonstrated to take place at the institutional and structural level – political intervention halted the labour movement's organisational reform initiative, as it would threaten the influence of the ruling elite over labour union decisions. The new cabinet headed by Salim al-Hoss decided to lift the demonstration ban[118] issued five years earlier by Hariri's cabinet (28 July 1993), and which prohibited demonstrations following the Israeli aggression.[119] The GCWL considered this decision a victory, as it had been demanding the removal of the ban for several years. The GCWL repeated its demands for a 30 per cent retroactive salary adjustment to take effect as of 1 January 1998 to take into account the increasing living expenses compared to 1996–98.[120] The year 1999 also witnessed the conflict surrounding the elections of the GCWL representatives to take up seats on the NSSF board, which is the major provider of social insurance coverage to workers and their family members in Lebanon. The social security system operated by the NSSF covers several categories of employees, including permanent employees in the formal private sector, employees in government-owned corporations, contractual and wage earners in public administration and teachers employed by private schools. The board was composed of stakeholder representatives of the state, business and trade union. In January 1999, the GCWL executive council organised elections of ten representatives for the NSSF board.[121] These elections were deemed illegal by several federations,[122] as elections had already been held under the previous executive council in 1997. They also criticised the elections for not taking into account the geographical distribution of federations.[123] Later on, the Ministry of Labour clarified that it had not issued a decree to endorse the previous election results. Soon after their election, the ten delegates declared the candidacy of Elias abu Rizq for the presidency of the NSSF board. On 19 March 1999, abu Rizq was voted into office as president of the NSSF board, beating Maurice Abu Nader to the post by three votes. This was the first time that a unionist leader had been elected to head up the NSSF board. The election of abu Rizq triggered a series of reactions from business associations which threatened to resign from the NSSF board. During the next month, abu Rizq called two board meetings but could not meet a quorum, as state and business representatives chose not to attend, in opposition to his election. On 16 April 1999, board members organised new elections and selected Maurice Abu Nader as the new president of the board.[124] Two days later, Elias abu Rizq announced his resignation as GCWL president, citing the interventions targeting the decision-making and independence of the GCWL. Technically his presidential mandate was scheduled to end six days later. Abu Rizq stayed on to head up the GCWL and was re-elected for another four-year mandate. The following December, abu Rizq was unanimously elected president of the executive council – with a council almost made up of the same members, including Yasir Ni'ma and Bassam Tlays.[125] Six opposing federations boycotted the first meeting of the GCWL for not receiving the meeting agenda.[126] The newly elected council first focused its attention on securing adequate representation of workers on the ESC.

The Ta'if Agreement had specified the creation of the ESC 'that guarantees the participation of representatives of the various sectors in the development of the economic and social policy of the country through the provision of guidance and recommendations'. Law No. 389 concerning the establishment of the ESC was enacted on 12 January 1995. The creation of the first governing body plus the election of the first executive bureau took place four years later in 1999.[127] The council's general assembly had a total of 71 members, which included 21 delegates to represent trade unions – the largest group in the assembly.

One main obstacle to the launch of the ESC was the nomination of representatives for the different bodies chosen by the Council of Ministers. The legitimacy of the ESC delegates rested on being nominated or elected by their respective organisations. In 2000, the GCWL clearly expressed disappointment with not being allowed to nominate its own representatives to the assembly.[128] Furthermore, the election of the ESC's executive bureau was also subject to government interference in the nomination of candidates. Elias abu Rizq denounced government meddling and resigned from the assembly in protest. In reality, abu Rizq had made a deal with Jacques Sarraf, the then president of the Association of Industrialists, to support each other in the election. The deal was for Sarraf to preside for one and a half years before resigning. Abu Rizq was to preside for the rest of the tenure.[129]

Following numerous delegates threatening to resign, the ESC elections were postponed. On 13 February 2000, Roger Nasnas was elected president of the executive bureau.[130] When the first mandate of the ESC expired in 2003, no new mandate was enacted and the council remained dormant until 2017 when Charles Arbid was voted in as president. The state's nomination of representatives to serve on the ESC and on its executive bureau exemplifies again the state's active repression of potential opposition or reform by manipulating the institutional framework.

A dormant movement: seventeen years and one only president

In August 2000, abu Rizq declared his candidacy in the forthcoming parliamentary elections for the South Lebanon governorate. When abu Rizq lost the elections, he announced his resignation as president of the GCWL.[131] Two days later, around forty unionists signed a petition requesting the executive council to meet and elect a new president, despite no official resignation having been submitted to the GCWL. Surprisingly, abu Rizq retracted his verbal resignation a few days later. In reaction to this, members of the executive bureau boycotted the meetings in September and October 2000, effectively forcing abu Rizq to cancel them. Abu Rizq remained president regardless of the actions taken by opposing federations. During this period, Prime Minister Salim al-Hoss resigned following his defeat in the parliamentary elections. Rafiq Hariri celebrated a landslide victory and was nominated prime minister for the fourth time.

In January 2001, abu Rizq inaugurated GCWL's new headquarters. The following six months were characterised by increasing tensions between members. After a series of negotiations, two-thirds of executive council members organised a meeting where they terminated the mandate of the executive bureau and called for elections to take place in March 2001.[132] On 15 March 2001, 47 out of 74 executive council members took part in the elections and unanimously chose Ghassan Ghusn to take the helm as president and Bassam Tlays as vice-president. As was to be expected – and as has since become the norm – members of the previous board, together with federations opposing the election winners, declared the elections illegal and did not recognise the results. Executive council members and the former executive bureau urged the Ministry of Labour to revoke the election results, but the request was rejected.[133] Ghassan Ghusn was now president of the GCWL and would remain so until 2017. The first year of the fifth executive bureau after the war was characterised by protests against the mass dismissal of workers, including employees of Middle East Airlines and Bonjus, one of the leading beverage and ice-cream producers in Lebanon founded in 1962. On 3 May 2001, MEA employees – the three trade unions representing employees, pilots and stewards – organised a strike at Beirut airport objecting to the likely dismissal of 1,440 workers considered redundant according to the reform plan aiming to privatise the company.[134] MEA workers and employees continued their protest on 21 and 22 June 2001, when they staged a sit-in at the company's premises and tried to break into the offices of its chairman, Mohammad al-Hut, demanding his resignation.[135] One month later, an agreement was reached between the company and MEA's ground workers, airline workers, employees and stewards.[136] The planned MEA restructuring also triggered the development of the NSSF voluntary scheme. Since a large number of employees and their dependants would be deprived of medical cover, a political decision was made to create the NSSF voluntary scheme to provide medical coverage for laid-off employees, knowing that social security only covered NSSF-registered employees and their dependants. The voluntary scheme lacked financial sustainability and soon accumulated a staggering deficit.[137]

Between July and October 2001, the union representing workers and employees of the juice company Bonjus took action and protested against the dismissal of workers. In July, 450 workers at Bonjus organised a strike at all company branches and warehouses in the south, north and the Bekaa. The company had already given notice to more than 180 employees. In October 2001, workers and employees of the Eternit cement company in North Lebanon organised a four-week strike to protest against delayed salary payments over the previous 30 months. At the beginning of 2002, the GCWL called for a mass demonstration on 28 February to repeat the demand for a wage adjustment and minimum wage increase by 30–40 per cent. However, after negotiating with Prime Minister Rafiq Hariri, the demonstration was called off. Surprisingly, the GCWL agreed with Hariri to accept the increase in transportation benefits from LBP 2,000 (US$1.3) to LBP 6,000 (US$4), and school fee benefits from LBP 1 million (US$660) to LBP 1.5 million (US$1,000), but abandoned the wage-increase claim.[138] In the end, the cabinet only passed the transport increase and postponed the enactment of school fees assistance.[139] In May 2004, the Government passed another fuel price increase, setting the cost of 20 litres at LBP 25,000 (US$16.5). The GCWL organised a set of demonstrations to which the Government responded by establishing a price ceiling of LBP 23,000 (US$15.3), even though the GCWL had demanded the price to be fixed at LBP 15,000 (US$10).[140] Later that month the GCWL called for another strike, together with a demonstration near the Council of Ministers' headquarters, to protest against the increasing prices and lack of social services. While the residents of Hay al-Sillum in the southern suburbs of Beirut were heading towards the main demonstration, the Lebanese army attempted to disperse the protest by shooting in the air using live ammunition. Protesters retaliated by throwing stones. The army shot at the unarmed protesters, killing five and injuring a dozen. The area was later declared a military zone and roads were blocked. As soon as the clashes began, the GCWL – the strike organiser – called on protesters to stop demonstrating and to remain peaceful. As the southern suburbs were Hezbollah strongholds, the party's Secretary-General Hassan Nasrallah made a public speech announcing that Hezbollah had been coordinating with the GCWL over the demonstration scheduled to take place in front of the Council of Ministers. He stated that an unnamed GCWL member had instructed protesters to act inside the southern suburbs and accused the American Embassy of having had a hand in the tragic events.[141] The GCWL's reaction was timid – it requested an investigation committee to be set up and called for a peaceful strike the following month in case negotiations did not produce positive results.[142] However, during the executive bureau meeting, LCP-affiliated members demanded that the GCWL take responsibility for the Hay al-Sillum events, which led to opposing stands and clashes among members.[143] On 16 June 2004, Hezbollah declared the resignation of trade unionists affiliated with Hezbollah from the GCWL's executive bureau, as it did not fulfil its commitment to the investigation of the Hay al-Sillum incident.[144] This event is an illustration of the role that political parties have played in steering the GCWL, which supersedes the needs and demands of the workforce. On 25 June 2004, a meeting was organised between the prime minister, business associations and the GCWL to discuss the workers' demands, most notably the increase in the minimum wage. Following the earlier positive discussions, when the Government and business associations had backed the launch of a tripartite dialogue to discuss wage increases, the GCWL revoked the call for strikes scheduled for 29 and 30 June 2004.[145] At this point, a group of federations established the Democratic Union Alliance as a response to the strike cancellation and to what they saw as a weak GCWL. On 23 August 2004, the GCWL organised the National Trade Unions Conference. The conference repeated the demands relating to adjusting wages that had been fixed at US$200 since 1996. The list of demands also included an increase in fringe benefits, the lowering of indirect taxation, strengthening and implementation of the NSSF, strict implementation of Article 50 of the Labour Code and the design of a housing policy, together with more support to the agriculture sector. The conference resulted in the formation of a committee tasked with following up on demands and setting a timeline for action.[146] The Government still did not respond to the GCWL's demands.

Rafiq Hariri was assassinated on 14 February 2005. People took to the streets – a series of demonstrations and rallies called for the end of Syrian occupation and blamed Syria together with President Émile Lahhud for the assassination of the prime minister. On 5 March, Syria's President Bashar Assad announced the redeployment of the Syrian army to the Bekaa and then to the border between Syria and Lebanon. On 8 March, Hezbollah called for a demonstration in support of Syria and accused Israel and the United States of intervening in Lebanese affairs. Hassan Nasrallah, the party leader, repeated his party's rejection of UN resolution 1559 requiring the dismantling of all militias. In turn, the anti-Syrian opposition called for a demonstration in central Beirut on 14 March to commemorate the assassination of Hariri and demand Syria's withdrawal from Lebanon, and an international inquiry into the assassination. During 2005, Lebanon witnessed a series of assassinations targeting political figures including the former secretary-general of the LCP, and journalists Samir Kassir and Gebran Tueini. On 26 April 2005, Syrian troops withdrew from Lebanon. Following the assassination of Hariri, the political divide was consolidated into two coalitions: March 14 and March 8. March 14 was a coalition of political parties that included the Free Patriotic Movement (FPM), Future Movement, the Lebanese Forces, the Phalanges Party, the PSP and the Democratic Left.[147] March 14 parties, led by the son of Rafiq Hariri, were united by their anti-Syrian stance. The March 8 alliance of parties was named after the demonstration that took place on 8 March 2005, when various political parties, notably Hezbollah and Amal, protested in central Beirut. It was a pro-Syrian rally expressing gratitude to the Syrian regime for its role during the civil war, while denouncing US and Israeli intervention in Lebanon. The March 8 coalition included al-Marada and the SSNP. In 2006, the FPM signed a memorandum of understanding with Hezbollah and became a de facto member of the March 8 coalition.

As a result of the political divisions resulting from Hariri's assassination, the GCWL was increasingly split between a March 8 leadership on the one hand – controlled by the Amal Party allied with Hezbollah – and the Democratic Union Alliance, that grouped communist and socialist party affiliates and independent GCWL members. The GCWL executive bureau's term ended in March 2005. Although its tenure had ended, the executive bureau authorised the admission of six new federations in April, just weeks before elections deciding the make-up of a new executive bureau. Out of the six federations, two were affiliated with Hezbollah and two others were linked to the Amal Movement.[148] The approval for the new federations to join was similar to the process that took place a few days before the 1997 and 1998 elections. Indeed, the last-minute authorisation of new federations immediately prior to elections had become common practice. It became the main tool used by the ruling elite, through the Ministry of Labour, to control the election results.

As expected, the federations rallying under the Democratic Union Alliance filed a lawsuit against the GCWL for admitting the six new federations. On 11 April, Judge Zalfa Hassan issued a ruling that revoked the decisions of the executive council's meeting of 5 April including the admission of the six new federations. Nevertheless, the Ministry of Labour annulled the judge's decision, referring to Labour Code Article 93. The elections took place as planned on 20 May 2005. During the counting of ballots, a bizarre incident took place – a young man sabotaged the election process by attacking the vote tellers before snatching the votes and escaping.[149] Two hours later, elections were conducted a second time, with the participation of 39 delegates out of a total of 66 delegates listed on the electoral roll.[150] Ghassan Ghusn was reappointed for another term with 36 votes, along with Vice-President Marun Khawli (35 votes) and treasurer Sa'd al-Din Saqr (37 votes). As had become a familiar practice, the opposition represented by the Democratic Union Alliance filed a lawsuit to annul the results as the election process was marred by illegal practices.[151] The rift within the labour movement was deepening and becoming increasingly acute.

Following the 34-day military conflict with Israel in 2006, an international donor conference known as Paris III was hosted by France in January 2007 to support Lebanon with debt servicing and the budgetary deficit. The Government presented an economic reform agenda aiming to reduce debt accumulation, lower poverty and stimulate economic growth. The reforms were based on six major pillars including growth-enhancing reforms, strengthening social safety nets, fiscal adjustments, privatisation and international financial assistance.[152] The GCWL immediately opposed the economic reform programme as it was enacted without consultation with the confederation, and it notably included additional taxes. The GCWL declared a series of sit-ins and demonstrations to begin outside the Value Added Tax Centre on 9 January 2007, followed by protests in front of the Ministry of Energy the next day, and then at the Ministry of Economy and Ogero headquarters[153] on 17 and 25 January, respectively. All these demonstrations saw a low turnout owing to the increasing divide within the labour movement. The reaction of the different federations and trade unions regarding the position of the GCWL mirrored the political rift between the ruling parties' March 14 political alliance and the March 8 coalition, made up of opposition parties. On one side, the March 14 coalition instructed workers and affiliated federations to boycott GCWL activities, accusing the confederation of being a creation of Syrian intervention. On the other side of the divide, the March 8 coalition supported the GCWL's stance against the prime minister's economic reform plan, which was mainly through the participation of Hezbollah and the Amal Movement in the GCWL sit-in, as both were central pillars of the March 8 coalition. The results were poor mobilisation and GCWL's failure to effectively stand against the Paris III economic reform agenda.[154] In November 2006, six Shiite ministers belonging to Hezbollah and their Amal allies resigned from the cabinet over attempts to disarm Hezbollah. Next, the Government was labelled illegitimate, because it did not include representatives from the Shiite community. Massive anti-government demonstrations followed in December 2006 calling for the resignation of Prime Minister Fu'ad Sanyura. By the end of President of the Republic Émile Lahhud's term in office in November 2007, no elections were held, leaving the position vacant and making the political crisis yet more complicated. The opposition parties were blocking the necessary quorum for presidential elections to pressure the Government to resign. The following February, in 2008, the GCWL declared the launch of a series of actions to demand a wage increase adjusting for the 63 per cent increase in living costs since 1996. However, the 7 May strike turned violent because of the protracted political crisis. That same day, fighting started between the March 8 and March 14 coalition forces, since the Government had made a decision on 6 May to shut down Hezbollah's telecommunication network plus remove Beirut Airport's security chief, Wafiq Shuqayr, over alleged ties to Hezbollah. Hezbollah leader, Hassan Nasrallah, declared the Government's dismantling of the party's telecommunications amounted to a 'declaration of war' and demanded that the Government restore the network. In Beirut, armed pro-Hezbollah protesters blocked roads with burning tyres, leaving the road towards Beirut Airport cut off. Riots swept across Beirut, resulting in heavy clashes between Hezbollah and the ruling majority. By the end of the day, March 8 forces, most notably Hezbollah, had completely occupied the streets of West Beirut and set up an armed blockade around the residences of the March 14 leaders, including Sa'ad Hariri, son of Rafiq Hariri. They vowed to continue until the Government backed down.

On 21 May, the Doha Agreement was reached and the rival Lebanese leaders agreed on steps to end the political deadlock – the ongoing governmental predicament and six months of presidential vacuum – that had led to the violent political crisis. A cabinet was formed, with 16 seats going to the ruling majority, who also got to select a prime minister, while 11 seats went to opposition representatives along with the power to veto decisions. Moreover, the elected president would nominate three cabinet seats. The parties agreed to ban the use of weapons in internal conflicts and the opposition protest camp in central Beirut was disbanded. However, the hardest part of the Doha negotiations was a new electoral law, which divided the country into smaller electoral districts based on the 1960 Law.

The GCWL continued to campaign for the minimum wage to be raised to LBP 960,000 (approximately US$645) as the cost of living had increased by another 15 per cent between 2006 and 2007. The confederation stressed that 40 per cent of the population was experiencing difficulties as their incomes had stagnated, while prices of most commodities had tripled during 2006 and 2007. In September 2008, the Government approved an increase of the monthly minimum wage from LBP 300,000 (US$200) to LBP 500,000 (US$333). Despite the difference between the stated demand and the actual increase that was passed, the confederation considered the wage increase to be in line with the tripartite negotiations that had taken place on 3 May 2008 and called it a victory for Lebanon's workers.[155]

Wage dispute and the ultimate failure of the GCWL

The beginning of the year saw Ghassan Ghusn's re-election for his fourth term as president of the GCWL. In June 2011, with the formation of a new Government, the confederation demanded a rise in the minimum wage (LBP 1,200,000, US$800) and Ghusn embarked on a series of meetings with the president of the republic and the justice and finance ministers, as well as chamber of commerce representatives. In September, the confederation announced a labour strike set for 12 October 2011 should the Government choose to ignore its demands.[156] The newly appointed Minister of Labour Charbel Nahas revived the PIC[157] as per Decree No. 4206 of 8 August 1981, and formed its new committee, composed of representatives of workers and business associations. As previously mentioned, Law No. 36 dating from 1967 stipulates that the Government of Lebanon is obliged to publish, via the PIC, a yearly cost-of-living index. Nevertheless, this committee had not convened for fifteen years since 1996 nor had there been any CPI-based wage increases during that period. It is important to note that the 1996 wage adjustment introduced for the first time a Government coping strategy to limit the wage increase: transport and education allowances were introduced as a temporary measure in a separate decree and were in turn considered not to be an integral part of workers' pay. Consequently, transport and education allowances were not included in the NSSF contribution paid by the employer, nor were they provided to informal workers, in the knowledge that Lebanon is characterised by a large informal sector. This strategy alleviates the financial burden on employers in general and the business elite in particular. These measures became permanent and this issue of transport allowances would continue to be a seminal negotiation point with business associations in future minimum wage policies, as shown in the sections below. Until 2008, the Government adopted no other wage adjustment. In September 2008, the Government implemented a wage adjustment, consisting of a flat increase to all monthly wages by LBP 200,000, backdated to May 2008. The minimum wage was hence increased from LBP 300,000 (US$200) to LBP 500,000 (US$333) by Decree No. 500. Similar to the 1996 rise, the Government issued Decree No. 501 relating to a daily transport allowance increase from LBP 6,000 to LBP 8,000. While the minimum wage became US$333, the average household income had to exceed US$500 to stay above the poverty line. Furthermore, as the rise was not linked to the consumer price index, it was not in proportion to the changes in the cost of living. This wage adjustment represents a 17 per cent average increase, in contrast to a 64 per cent increase in the general consumer price index between 1996 and 2008. As long as transport allowances were not integrated into the minimum wage, increases in these were deducted from NSSF. Despite the difference between the voiced demand and the increase that was passed, the co-opted GCWL considered the wage increase a victory for workers. In 2011 the question of wages was raised again. After deliberations among stakeholders during two consecutive PIC meetings, data analysis showed that the CPI increased by 100 per cent between 1996 and 2011. During the same period, transport fees were four times higher, whereas wages had only increased by 16 per cent instead of 121 percent, based on calculated price rises during that period.[158] At this point the GCWL proposed to raise the minimum wage to LBP 1,250,000 to boost wages, following a progressive scale. The proposal considered 1996 as the baseline for price-increase calculations to reconsider transport allowances and school assistance. Business associations instead wanted to consider 2008 as the starting point for raising the minimum wage, and thus proposed to raise it by 16 per cent, corresponding to the rise in the cost of living since 2008.

The minister had put together a reform package that aimed to ensure a periodic adjustment of wages in accordance with Law No. 36, integrating transport allowances into wages and increasing salaries by 20 per cent with a ceiling of LBP 1,500,000 (US$1,000). He also planned to tax real-estate transactions and revive the role of trade unions. The reform package also included a strategy for the creation of a universal healthcare scheme in Lebanon. Incorporating transport allowances into people's wages also aimed to protect 45 per cent of employees in Lebanon that were not granted such an allowance.[159] However, the package of reforms assembled by the Ministry of Labour was not put on the agenda at the upcoming Council of Ministers.[160] Instead the Council of Ministers approved a proposal illegitimately put forward by Prime Minister Najib Miqati. Lebanon's prime minister is not entitled to present a wage proposal, as this instead falls under the prerogative of the minister of labour. The proposal suggested a minimum wage rise from LBP 500,000 (US$333) to LBP 700,000 (US$460) and an increase in daily transport allowances to LBP 10,000. The GCWL not only relinquished the opportunity to champion the social reforms package presented by Nahas but was also quick to cancel the strike signalling acceptance of the prime minister's proposal. However, in its ruling from 27 October 2011, the State Shura Council – one of Lebanon's highest judicial authorities – found that the Government's decision was unlawful on several grounds. The principal reason was that it did not comprise a cost-of-living index justifying the proposed wage increase as per Law No. 36.[161] On 21 December, Nahas planned to present a revised wage proposal to the Council of Ministers. But while the Council of Ministers were meeting, Prime Minister Miqati and President of the Republic Michel Suleiman were holding a parallel meeting. They had invited representatives of business associations and the GCWL to convene in a nearby room and were facilitating an agreement on a minimum wage rise with the parties present. As soon as the agreement was signed, Miqati walked into the cabinet meeting and declared that the discussion and vote on Minister of Labour Naha's proposal was no longer needed since business associations and the GCWL had already agreed on a new minimum wage. Miqati's minimum wage agreement yielded much less for workers – it granted LBP 675,000 (US$450) instead of GCWL's initial demand of LBP 1,200,000 (US$800),[162] or the CPI-based minimum wage of LBP 800,000 (US$533).[163] At this point, Nahas refused to discuss Miqati's deal and strongly insisted on respecting the meeting agenda – a new agreement should only be considered after his proposal had been debated and voted on. Nahas won the cabinet vote this time. His proposal provided for a 74 per cent increase up from LBP 500,000 (US$333) to LBP 868,000 (US$580). Nahas referred his proposal to the State Shura Council, but the court rejected it on the basis that transport allowances are illegal and the Council of Ministers only had the power to adjust wages. The court requested the removal of the article pertaining to the transport allowance.

Meanwhile, the GCWL and business associations were insisting on the implementation of their 21 December agreement, whereas Nahas and the Union Coordination Committee (UCC), a coalition of public-sector employees, rejected the deal because it was informal and the transportation allowance component was unlawful. The UCC stressed the importance of abiding by Decree-Law No. 36 and Law No. 138. The minister of labour also insisted that the existence of a transport allowance was not only unlawful but irrelevant because the Council of Ministers only had the power to adjust wages. This point was confirmed by the State Shura Council. With this justification, and reasoning that 45 per cent of workers did not benefit from these payments, the court cancelled all previous decrees relating to transport and education allowances. On 18 January 2012, the Council of Ministers again voted on Nahas's proposal. It included the same figures but without proposing any transport allowances. Out of 30 ministers, 29 voted against Nahas's proposal, including members of his own ministerial coalition. On 25 January 2012, Decree No. 7426 was adopted, increasing the monthly minimum wage for private-sector employees from LBP 500,000 (US$333) to LBP 675,000 (US$450) and providing for a living cost increase up to LBP 299,000 (US$200) per month.

Prime Minister Miqati went on to ask for a decree reinstating the transport allowance, despite the State Shura Council's previous ruling on the issue. Miqati insisted, but Nahas refused to sign a second decree relating to transportation allowances, contending that it was unlawful and a violation of workers' rights.[164] In response, Prime Minister Miqati suspended cabinet meetings until Nahas agreed to sign the decree. Nahas resigned on 21 February 2012 and the decree was signed immediately thereafter by acting Minister of Labour Nicolas Fattush.[165] The episode shows the absurd behaviour of the GCWL. The GCWL surprisingly sided with business associations in approving the deal offered by the prime minister and opposed the much better deal put on the table by the minister of labour. The political coalition to which Minister of Labour Nahas belonged voted against his proposal – puzzling actions, given that they paved the way for a deal proposed by their political opponent Prime Minister Miqati. The coalition's quick political flip was a result of an alleged secret bargain between the coalition leader Michel Aoun and Nabih Berri who by then had successfully co-opted the GCWL.[166] In the end, the Decree-Law No. 7426 was passed, despite the State Shura Council's judicial review ruling it to be unlawful. A closer look also shows how a fair wage proposal failed as it ran counter to the strategic interests of the ruling elite who agreed and planned together on how to obstruct the proposal becoming law. The episode clearly shows how the GCWL had become completely severed from the interests of the workers it claimed to represent. In summary, the labour movement's trajectory during the post-war period was mostly a continuation of its path before and during the war. The demands of the labour movement were restricted to working and living conditions and did not go beyond to call for fundamental reforms. How and why was the labour movement co-opted and what were the repercussions on Lebanon's sectarian-liberal model? First, the affiliations of the GCWL leadership mirrored the political alliances at the state level. The mobilisation of the GCWL was more a reflection of political tensions and conflicts between political stakeholders than manifestations of workers' demands. GCWL members' voting was directed by clear instructions given by the political parties.

Second, the post-war period witnessed state intervention on a larger scale. It was through the authorisation of additional federations that the Ministry of Labour succeeded in controlling the GCWL. The main strategy used by the ruling elite to co-opt the labour movement was to grant an excessive number of authorisations to union federations through the Ministry of Labour. The elections of loyalist trade unionists were secured through political intervention and pressure that tapped into the political and sectarian affiliations of trade unionists.

Third, the Syrian presence in Lebanon and its interference in Lebanese internal politics also played a significant role in reducing the influence and power of the labour movement. Taking into account the importance of labour issues for political stability and control, the Ministry of Labour minister posts had primarily been assigned to political parties that were close to the Syrian regime. The Ministry of Labour's interference in GCWL decisions, actions and elections was a necessary tool to manage political stability in the country. Finally, the elite successfully redirected state resources towards the banking sector and private interests. The effects of crowding out on the private sector and the economic recession at the end of the 1990s harmed employment and exacerbated social inequalities. As a result of the crowding-out effect, the Lebanese economy was reduced to only small-sized enterprises and a few industrial enterprises. This predominance of micro- and small-scale businesses is one of the key factors behind the low numbers of unionised workers in Lebanon. In conclusion, what is often perceived as the fall of the labour movement, following the civil war, was in fact an intensification of the already existing influence of political parties, state intervention and co-optation, and the effects of liberal economic policies. Beyond controlling the labour movement to avoid a challenge to the overall system and ensure political stability, the co-optation of the GCWL also served as a tool in the disputes of the elites over power, rents and benefits. The co-optation of the labour movement guaranteed the absence of opposition and a political alternative to the sectarian-liberal system in place. Breaking labour power was essential to maintain the system and to curb opposition.

In fact, the successful control of the labour movement during this period explains the absence of labour power that could effectively oppose the harsh sectarian-liberal system in October 2019 at a time when people came together to fight for change and a new political system. The 2019 October uprising faced the same obstacles as the labour movement in the early 1990s; however, at this point, the labour movement had been fully manipulated and outmanoeuvred and was no longer an ally capable of fighting for workers' rights.

Notes

1 H. Baumann, 'Social protest and the political economy of sectarianism in Lebanon', *Global Discourse* (8 December 2016), p. 2.
2 *Ibid.*, p. 14.
3 Makdisi, *The Culture of Sectarianism*, p. xi.
4 S. Ofeish, 'Lebanon's second republic: secular talk, sectarian application', *Arab Studies Quarterly*, 21:1 (1999), 106–7.
5 *Ibid.*, pp. 105–6.
6 Messarra, *La Structure Sociale du Parlement Libanais (1920–1976)*, p. 57.
7 Since 1968, all presidents of the GCWL have been Christian Maronites except for Elias abu Rizq, who was Christian Orthodox. GCWL Presidents up to 2020 were as follows: Gabriel Khouri (1968–73); Georges Saqr (1973–83); Antoine Bishara (1983–93); Elias abu Rizq (1993–97); Ghanim al-Zughbi (1997–98); Elias abu Rizq (1998–2000); Ghassan Ghusn (2000–17); Bishara al-Asmar (2017–20).
8 *As-Safir* (21 January 1983), p. 9.
9 *As-Safir* (29 January 1983), p. 9.
10 Since the GCWL presidency is traditionally held by Christians, the vice-presidency became informally allocated to Shiites, given that federations affiliated to Amal and Hezbollah constitute the majority of federations of the GCWL. Ghassan Slaiby, interviewed by Lea Bou Khater, 10 October 2020.
11 On the subject see F. el-Khazen, 'Lebanon's first postwar parliamentary elections, 1993', *Middle East Policy*, 3:1 (1994), 120.
12 On the subject see F. Kiwan, 'Forces politiques nouvelles, système politique ancien' in F. Kiwan and A. Beydoun (eds), *Le Liban Aujourd'hui* (Beirut: CERMOC, 1994).
13 Kiwan and Beydoun (eds), *Le Liban Aujourd'hui*.
14 J. Bahout and C. Douayhi, *La vie Publique au Liban: Expressions et Recompositions du Politique* (Beirut: CERMOC, 1997), p. 24.
15 J. Chalcraft, *The Invisible Cage: Syrian Migrant Workers in Lebanon* (Stanford, CA: Stanford University Press, 2009).
16 F. Balanche, 'Les travailleurs syriens au Liban ou la complémentarité de deux systèmes d'oppression', *Le Monde Diplomatique* (Arabic edition), March 2007.
17 G. Gambill, 'Syrian workers in Lebanon: the other occupation', *Middle East Intelligence Bulletin*, February 2001.
18 ILO, *Towards Decent Work in Lebanon: Issues and Challenges in Light of the Syrian Refugee Crisis* (Beirut: ILO, 2015).
19 Chalcraft, *The Invisible Cage*, p. 142.
20 Abdallah al-Amin, 1992–95, Baath Party; As'ad Hirdan 1995–98, SSNP; Michel Mussa, 1998–2000, Amal Party; Ali Qansu, 2000–03, SSNP; As'ad Hirdan, 2003–04, SSNP; 'Asim Qanso, 2004–05, Baath Party.
21 The CDR was created in 1977 to supervise the reconstruction of infrastructure and raise funds from donors.

22 M. Retting, 'The Role of the Banking Sector in the Economic Process of Lebanon, before and after the Civil War' (Master's dissertation, School of Oriental and African Studies, London, 2004).

23 T. Addison and P. Le Billon, 'Finance in conflict and reconstruction', *University and World Institute for Development Economics Research*, 44 (2001).

24 K. Dib, *Warlords and Merchants: The Lebanese Business and Political Establishment* (Reading: Ithaca Press, 2004), pp. 91–2.

25 Ministry of Finance, *Public Finance Yearly Report 2011* (Beirut: Ministry of Finance, 2011).

26 Gaspard, *A Political Economy of Lebanon*, p. 90.

27 *Ibid.*, p. 92.

28 Retting, 'The Role of the Banking Sector in the Economic Process of Lebanon, before and after the Civil War'.

29 S. Baroudi, 'Continuity in economic policy in postwar Lebanon: the record of the Hariri and Hoss governments examined, 1992–2000', *Arab Studies Quarterly*, 24: 1 (2002), 63.

30 K. Hamdan, 'Micro and small enterprises in Lebanon', *Policy Research Report Series* (Cairo: Economic Research Forum, 2004).

31 CAS, *L'enquête par Sondage pour la Population Active au Liban 1970* (Beirut: CAS, 1972); CAS, *Multiple Indicators Cluster Survey 2009* (Beirut: CAS, 2010).

32 C. Kasparian, *L'émigration des Jeunes Libanais et leurs Projets d'Avenir: Les Jeunes Libanais Dans La Vague D'emigration de 1992 à 2007*, Volume 2 (Beirut: Presses de l'Universite Saint-Joseph, 2009), pp. 19–20.

33 World Bank, *Republic of Lebanon – Good Jobs Needed: The Role of Macro, Investment, Education, Labor and Social Protection Policies* (Washington, DC: World Bank, 2012).

34 Examining reports from the biannual National Trade Unions Conference shows that it was largely the same package of demands, which was repeatedly put forward.

35 Rafiq al-Hariri was both prime minister and minister of finance between 1992 and 1998. Fu'ad al-Sanyura was minister of finance in charge during this period.

36 He was appointed minister of finance in 2000.

37 OGER is a private construction company established in 1978 and is solely owned by the Hariri family.

38 S. Srouji, 'Capturing the State: A Political Economy of Lebanon's Public Debt Crisis 1992–2004' (Master's dissertation, Institute of Social Studies, The Hague, 2005).

39 *Société Libanaise pour le Développement et la Reconstruction* (Lebanese Society for Development and Reconstruction).

40 Corm, *Le Liban Contemporain*, pp. 249–50; G. Corm, 'La reconstruction de Beyrouth: un exemple de fièvre immobilière au Liban', *Revue d'Economie Financière*, December 1993.

41 Baroudi, 'Economic conflict in postwar Lebanon', 532; *An-Nahar* (2 May 1993), p. 11.

42 *An-Nahar* (8 July 1993), p. 9.
43 *An-Nahar* (9 July 1993). p. 8.
44 *An-Nahar* (15 May 1997). p. 9.
45 Baroudi, 'Economic conflict in postwar Lebanon', 532.
46 *Ibid.*, 544.
47 *Ibid.*, 545.
48 The final conference document repeated the demands for wage increases, addi-
    tional worker benefits, enhanced control over consumer prices, a progressive
    taxation system, additional public spending on education and health services, a
    new salary scale for professors from the Lebanese University and schoolteachers,
    establishing the ESC as stipulated in the Ta'if Agreement, and the endorsement
    of the prerogatives of the GCWL to name its representatives to the ESC. GCWL,
    'Taqrir mu'tamar al-naqabi al-watani al-'am 1994' (13 December 1994).
49 *As-Safir* (26 February 1996), p. 6; *An-Nahar* (22 August 1996), p. 14;
    An-Nahar (30 August 1996), p. 10.
50 *An-Nahar* (15 May 1997), p. 11.
51 GCWL, 'Taqrir mu'tamar al-naqabi al-watani al-'am 1996'; *As-Safir*
    (7 February 1996), p. 6.
52 *As-Safir* (10 February 1996), p. 2; *Al-Hayat* (5 March 1996), p. 6.
53 The PIC includes representatives of business associations, the GCWL and
    the Ministry of Labour to determine annual wage increases in line with the
    increase of cost of goods and services.
54 *As-Safir* (13 March 1996), p. 3.
55 *An-Nahar* (27 March 1996).
56 The visit of President Jacques Chirac to Lebanon was an important event
    for Hariri, who had had a close relationship with him since the 1980s.
    Furthermore, some observers accused Hariri of financing Chirac's election
    campaign in 1995. Other critics noted that the close relationship between the
    two men was behind the French support for the donors' conference organised
    in France in 2002 (Paris II). Hannes Baumann, 'Citizen Hariri and Neoliberal
    Politics in Postwar Lebanon' (PhD dissertation, School of Oriental and African
    Studies, London, 2012).
57 *An-Nahar* (4 April 1996), p. 2.
58 The national gathering (Al Lika' al-Watani) was a meeting of opposition
    leaders including Hussein el Husseini, Salim al-Huss and representatives of the
    Phalanges Party and the LCP.
59 *An-Nahar* (26 September 1996).
60 The Amal Movement was founded in 1974 as the 'Movement of the
    Dispossessed'. It is associated with the Shiite community and is represented
    in Parliament with thirteen deputies (2016). Since 1980 Amal's chairman has
    been Nabih Birri. He has been president of Parliament since October 1992.
61 *An-Nahar* (13 May 1998), p. 13.
62 This federation would also be subject to division. On 11 May 1997, despite the
    elections that took place on 13 April, the federation would witness the election
    of a second executive council.

63 *As-Safir* (17 April 1997), p. 13; *As-Safir* (18 April 1997), p. 12.
64 The GCWL had required the five federations to submit additional documents in order to complete their application. *As-Safir* (17 April 1997), p. 15.
65 *An-Nahar* (15 May 1997), p. 9.
66 Article 93 of the Labour Code states: 'Applications for membership is presented to the trade union committee together with the identity card and a work certificate approved by the Social Affairs Services and indicating that the Applicant carries on the profession represented by the trade union. Within fifteen days, the trade union committee must decide by secret ballot whether the Applicant is to be admitted or refused'; Article 94: 'The applicant may object to the refusal decision before the Social Affairs Service which then adjudicates his case.' Translation of the 'Code of Labour', *Argus de la legislation Libanaise*, 56:1 (First quarter 2010), 19. During an interview, Elias abu Rizq pointed out that these articles refer to the admittance of working individuals and not to federations and therefore were irrelevant to the 1997 election case.
67 *As-Safir* (17 April 1997), p. 12.
68 The Federation of workers in metal, mechanics and electronics, the Lebanese Federation of taxi drivers and transport institutions in Lebanon, the national Federation of workers and employees in South Lebanon and the Federation for agricultural workers in Jabal 'Amil.
69 *As-Safir* (17 April 1997), p. 12.
70 *An-Nahar* (24 April 1997), p. 12. The GCWL executive bureau refused to submit the list of federation delegates to the executive council, as requested by the Ministry of Labour based on Decree No. 52/7993 to supervise the elections. Therefore, one day before the elections the ministry published the list of delegates of the 27 delegations eligible to participate in the bureau elections. It is important to note that during the 1993 elections, the GCWL did not submit a list of delegates to the Ministry of Labour but only disclosed the delegates to its representatives on election day.
71 *Addiyar* (25 April 1997), p. 11.
72 *An-Nahar* (15 May 1997), p. 10.
73 Al-Zughbi had participated in trade union work since 1964 within the trade Union of workers and employees of water authorities in Lebanon. He took part in the establishment of the Federation of trade unions of independent authorities and public and private institutions, of which he became secretary-general and later its representative on the GCWL executive council. *An-Nahar* (29 April 1997), p. 9.
74 *Ibid.*
75 'What happened in the elections was very disappointing and has led, as expected, to the dangerous split of the labour movement. All this is due to the clear and unjustified interference of the Government in these elections and its direct support to one party against another.' *An-Nahar* (29 April 1997), p. 9.
76 *An-Nahar* (26 April 1997), p. 11.
77 *An-Nahar* (25 April 1997), p. 1.
78 *An-Nahar* (29 April 1997), p. 9.

79 *An-Nahar* (24 July 1997), p. 1. During a television interview in 1997, Rafiq
    Hariri revealed for the first time that the security forces had indeed intervened
    in the 1997 GCWL elections.

80 ESC, NSSF, the Consumer Index Committee and the National Employment
    Office (NEO).

81 *An-Nahar* (16 May 1997), pp. 8–10.

82 *An-Nahar* (26 April 1997), p. 11.

83 I. Badran and M. Zbib, *al-Ittihad al-'Ummali al-'Am fi Lubnan* (Beirut:
    Friedrich-Ebert-Stiftung, 2004). Political parties such as the Baath Party and
    the SSNP were actively trying to increase their influence on the workers' move-
    ment in the early post-war period.

84 Baumann, 'Citizen Hariri and Neoliberal Politics in Postwar Lebanon'.

85 My calculations are based on Ministry of Labour data. Prior to every election,
    every trade union is required to submit a list of its members to the Ministry of
    Labour. This is a legal requirement of the ministry in order for it to endorse
    election results. The Ministry of Labour is supposed to hold the updated details
    of all active trade unions. The ministry's data pertaining to federations and
    trade unions are not computerised but are archived in folders that contain
    information classified by the Federation of trade unions. The most recent
    number of trade union members can only be found for the year of the last
    board election. Trade unions can have irregular elections and the number of
    members recorded in the electoral list can therefore date from a considerable
    number of years ago.

86 Bu Habib (2014), interview; Ahmad Dirani (2014), interviewed by Lea Bou
    Khater, 10 August. Dirani is the director of the Lebanese Observatory for the
    Rights of Workers and Employees.

87 Bu Habib (2014), interview; Mohamad Zbib (2013), interviewed by Lea Bou
    Khater, 23 October. Mohammad Zbib is a journalist, former senior eco-
    nomics editor at the Lebanese newspaper *al-Akhbar*; Ghassan Slaybi (2014)
    interviewed by Lea Bou Khater, 20 October. Ghassan Slaybi was a former
    researcher at the GCWL. He is an international expert in union training and
    the regional coordinator for the International Union of Public Service Workers.

88 Badran and Zbib, *Al-Ittihad al-'Ummali al-'Am fi Lubnan*.

89 Ghassan Slaybi (2014); Mohamad Zbib (2013).

90 Badran and Zbib, *Al-Ittihad al-'Ummali al-'Am fi Lubnan*.

91 Drawing upon these substantial limitations, the numbers used in the section
    below should be considered with caution (see the Introduction). Yearly com-
    parisons are difficult as data are collected from different sources due to the lack
    of consolidated official numbers. In 2015, the number of trade unions that had
    conducted elections in the previous five years was 268. The last elections were
    held in 2010. My calculations are based on data collected from the Ministry of
    Labour.

92 Badran and Zbib, *al-Ittihad al-'Ummali al-'Am fi Lubnan*. Labour force
    surveys in Lebanon are not produced in a systematic and consistent way, which
    inhibits the possibility of identifying a long-term trend. These findings aim to

describe the true situation, but it is important to note these limitations, as well as problems of reliability regarding official statistics.

93 *An-Nahar* (1 May 1997), p. 11. These were the federations of trade unions of workers and employees in printing and the media, construction and carpentry and taxi drivers in land transport.

94 Decision issued on 15 May 1997; *An-Nahar* (16 May 1997), p. 8.

95 *An-Nahar* (22 May 1997), p. 10.

96 *An-Nahar* (31 May 1997), p. 10.

97 *An-Nahar* (2 June 1997), p. 11.

98 *An-Nahar* (6 May 1997), p. 11. Former Prime Minister Omar Karami, members of Parliament: Elias Skaff, Mohammad Fnaysh and Albert Mukhayber.

99 *An-Nahar* (9 June 1997), p. 1.

100 The Hunger Revolution was called for and organised by Sheikh Subhi al-Tufayyli, who was a Hezbollah spokesman between 1985 and 1989 and sec-retary-general from 1989 to 1991. He split from Hezbollah in 1992 in protest against the decision of the party to participate in parliamentary elections. The Hunger Revolution was criticised for merely being a reflection of the split within the party.

101 *An-Nahar* (4 July 1997), p. 9.

102 *An-Nahar* (14 November 1997), p. 11; *An-Nahar* (15 November 1997), p. 10.

103 The General Director of Port of Beirut Mulhim 'Itani requested the unionists at the grain silos to arrive one hour ahead of their usual starting time. Issam al-Jurdi, *Mahattat al-Inkisam fi al-Ittihad al-'Ummali al-'am* (Beirut: LCPS, 1998).

104 *An-Nahar* (25 November 1997), p. 14.

105 *An-Nahar* (23 January 1998), p. 6.

106 *An-Nahar* (27 January 1998), p. 6.

107 *An-Nahar* (3 February 1998), p. 8.

108 *An-Nahar* (25 February 1998), p. 9.

109 *An-Nahar* (13 February 1998), p. 10.

110 *An-Nahar* (13 May 1998), p. 6.

111 *An-Nahar* (12 March 1998), p. 10.

112 Talal Hajjar was a member of the Trade union of electricity workers while Shawki Ismail was part of the Trade union of Ogero employees.

113 *An-Nahar* (1 April 1998), p. 10.

114 *An-Nahar* (28 July 1998), p. 8.

115 *An-Nahar* (31 July 1998), p. 1. The executive council was composed of 56 delegates that represented 28 federations. Out of the 56 members, 52 attended the elections, 32 voted for Elias abu Rizq and 3 voted for Georges Harb. White ballots amounted to 11, while 5 ballots were cancelled. Walid al-Jurdi, vice-president of the Federation of the South, did not attend the session as he was a strong supporter of Prime Minister Hariri. He continued to boycott the activi-ties of the GCWL under abu Rizq's leadership.

116 The memorandum focused on the protection of public, trade union and media freedoms, the annulment of the demonstration ban, an end to privatisation, the

enactment of the ESC, protection of the Lebanese labour force and protection of the NSSF plus wage adjustments.

117 *An-Nahar* (16 May 1995), p. 8.

118 The ban was lifted on 22 December 1998.

119 'In order to protect the security of citizens and in light of military events, gatherings and demonstrations are prohibited to take place on Lebanese territory, and security and armed forces are assigned to enforce this decision.' (Author's translation.)

120 *An-Nahar* (22 January 1998), p. 8.

121 *An-Nahar* (2 February 1999), p. 10. Ghazi al-Hibri, Ghassan Ghusn, Elias abu Rizq, Fadlallah Sharif, Joseph Youssef, Halim Matar, Jihad al-Muʿallem, Georges ʿAlam, Hussein Ali Hussein and Slayman Hamdan.

122 Including the federations of workers and employees of South Lebanon and North Lebanon.

123 Article 2 of the NSSF Code and article 2 of Decree-Law No. 2390 dated 1992 stipulates that: 'The GCWL is considered the most representative body for employees on Lebanese territories and is responsible to choose 10 delegates [to the NSSF board] taking into account the representation of all governorates.'

124 *An-Nahar* (17 April 1999), p. 8.

125 *An-Nahar* (17 December 1999), p. 10. 49 delegates represented 25 federations and voted unanimously for the new executive board.

126 *An-Nahar* (13 January 2000), p. 10. The federations of banks, trade transport, workers' unions, free unions and of workers of South Lebanon.

127 Implementation decrees were issued in 2000 and the designation of the official headquarters took place in 2002.

128 *An-Nahar* (22 January 2000), p. 8.

129 *An-Nahar* (26 January 2000), p. 9. Abu Rizq had opposed the election of Roger Nasnas, director of Axa Insurance, for the presidency of ESC. He declared that the presidency should not be awarded to employers. Later on, it was said that the Catholic Patriarch in Beirut recommended the election of a president from the Catholic community since it was underrepresented in government.

130 *An-Nahar* (14 February 2000), p. 6.

131 Abu Rizq announced his resignation on 4 September 2000.

132 *An-Nahar* (21 February 2001), p. 8.

133 *An-Nahar* (22 March 2001), p. 8.

134 The reform plan was agreed by the cabinet and dated 8 March 2001. *An-Nahar* (5 May 2001), p. 7.

135 *An-Nahar* (22 June 2001), p. 13.

136 *An-Nahar* (4 July 2001); *An-Nahar* (24 July 2001).

137 F. el-Jardali et al., 'A retrospective health policy analysis of the development and implementation of the voluntary health insurance system in Lebanon: learning from failure', *Social Science and Medicine*, 123 (2014), 45–54.

138 *An-Nahar* (26 February 2002), p. 1.

139 *An-Nahar* (1 March 2002), p. 1.

140 *An-Nahar* (21 May 2004), pp. 15–16.

141 *An-Nahar* (28 May 2004), p. 13; *An-Nahar* (30 May 2004), p. 15.
142 GCWL, 'Bayan sadir 'an al-majlis al-tanfizi lil-ittihad al-'ummali al-'am' (28 May 2004).
143 *An-Nahar* (11 June 2004), p. 16.
144 *An-Nahar* (17 June 2004), p. 18.
145 *An-Nahar* (28 June 2004), p. 15.
146 *An-Nahar* (24 August 2004), p. 16.
147 The FPM left the alliance after the 2005 parliamentary elections. The PSP left the 14 March coalition in 2011.
148 *An-Nahar* (6 April 2005), p. 15; *An-Nahar* (11 April 2005), p. 13. The Federation of loyalty to the trade unions of transport (affiliated with Hezbollah), the general Federation of sectorial trade unions, the Federation of workers and employees in Baalbek-Hermel (affiliated with Hezbollah), the Federation of workers and employees in Beirut, the Federation of technical unions (affiliated with Amal) and the Federation of unions of workers in cooperatives and vegetable markets in Lebanon (affiliated with Amal). The six new federations were affiliated with the Shiite community.
149 *An-Nahar* (21 May 2005), p. 15. The son of Mohammad Jamal Shihab, a candidate running for the post of GCWL secretary-general, was accused of being the perpetrator.
150 *Ibid.* Before polling day, the GCWL submitted an electoral roll listing 23 out of 36 federations allowed to participate in the elections. However, during the elections, the electoral roll appeared to include 33 federations.
151 *An-Nahar* (27 May 2005), p. 16.
152 Lebanese Republic, 'Recovery, Reconstruction, and Reform: International Conference for Support to Lebanon, Paris, 25 January 2007' (Beirut, 2007).
153 Ogero is the main fixed telecommunications network operator, working on behalf of the Lebanese Ministry of Telecommunications.
154 *An-Nahar* (9 January 2007), p. 14; *An-Nahar* (10 January 2007), p. 10; *An-Nahar* (11 January 2007), p. 15; *An-Nahar* (17 January 2007), pp. 13–14; *An-Nahar* (18 January 2007), p. 8.
155 *An-Nahar* (11 September 2008), p. 15.
156 *An-Nahar* (6 June 2011), p. 14; *An-Nahar* (7 September June 2011), p. 13.
157 The PIC was set up on 23 September 2011.
158 PIC, 'Report of the second meeting', 2011.
159 World Bank, *Republic of Lebanon – Good Jobs Needed*.
160 The Council of Ministers meeting took place on 11 October 2011.
161 Opinion No. 23 dated 27 October 2011. Article 6 of Law No. 36.
162 *An-Nahar* (29 December 2011), p. 13.
163 PIC, 'Report of the Price Index Committee, Part II' (Beirut, 18 January 2012). The report valued the CPI-based minimum wage at LBP 816,000 (US$540).
164 State Shura Council, 'State Shura Council Opinion 95/2012'. The State Shura Council had found that the transportation allowance decrees adopted by the consecutive Lebanese cabinets were unlawful and that the cabinet had no jurisdiction to issue such decrees.

165 Decree No. 7426 dated 25 January 2012; *An-Nahar* (21 January 2012), p. 13; Ministry of Finance, 'Lebanon country profile 2013' (Beirut: Ministry of Finance, 2013). Nahas explained that a member of Parliament from his coalition paid him a visit to deliver a message from Michel Aoun, head of the coalition and president of the FPM, directing him to sign the decree immediately or resign.

166 According to Nahas, a dinner was arranged between the two men where a deal was made whereby Aoun agreed not to implement Nahas's wage-increase proposals. It is not clear what was Aoun offered in exchange.

3

Public-sector employees gear up

Amid the protracted paralysis of the GCWL, the labour movement in Lebanon showed signs of revival in 2011 with a ground-breaking mobilisation of public-sector employees who rallied under the UCC to demand a wage adjustment.[1] This chapter first examines the obstacles to public-sector mobilisation plus the UCC's structural resilience to help better understand its actions and extensive movement. The second part of the chapter explains the main organising features of the UCC, notably the relationship between the UCC and the Government. The chapter aims to answer the following questions: in light of the scanty results of the private-sector trade unions, how can the resilience and effective mobilisation of the public sector be explained? And what impact did sectarian affiliations have on the functioning and performance of the UCC?

Facing lay-off threats in 2012, 1,800 daily contracted workers together with 700 contracted collectors at Electricité du Liban stopped working for 94 continuous days and organised sit-ins at the company headquarters.[2] In 2012, a group of workers at the supermarket chain Spinneys mobilised against their employer, which had refused to implement a new law (Law No. 7426) that decreed an increase to the minimum wage. They called for strikes and demonstrations and set up a workers' union and were, as a consequence, harassed and subjected to arbitrary dismissals. In March 2013, the Federation of trade unions of bank workers and employees started to exert pressure on the Association of Banks in Lebanon by organising sit-ins in different regions of the country. The federation's demands mainly consisted of a collective labour contract that preserved the acquired rights of employees, a wage increase, and the provision of healthcare coverage for retirees. Workers in the banking sector, accounting for 25,000 employees, are the only workers in Lebanon to benefit from a collective contract and were facing an attempt by the Association of Banks in Lebanon to strip away this bargaining power.[3] In January 2015, a union for domestic workers in Lebanon – the first union of its kind in the Arab world – was created, despite the opposition of the Ministry of Labour.[4]

Nevertheless, the most significant action during this period was the three-year mobilisation calling for a new public-sector salary scale demanded by the UCC, a coalition of the League of primary public school teachers, the League of secondary public school teachers, the Trade union of private school teachers and the League of public-sector employees. The organisation and mobilisation of public-sector workers came as a reaction to the dormant and highly politicised GCWL.

A long-standing tradition

Coordination committees, as a vehicle of trade union activism in Lebanon, are not a recent phenomenon. Prior to the outbreak of the civil war in 1975, they existed in various forms and with different structures. In the 1970s, a coordination committee of public-sector workers represented teachers as well as public-sector employees and actively sought the establishment of public schools and the provision of water, electricity and telephone lines, benefiting all regions in Lebanon. In the early 1990s, the Bureau of Teachers, which coordinated the actions of the various independent teacher leagues, joined forces with the GCWL and formed the UCC. In addition to lobbying for workers' rights, the newly established body advocated an end to the war.[5]

In the post-war era, the coalition made up of leagues of teachers and civil servants took action against contractual arrangements in the public sector, the rolling back of the welfare state, and the erosion of the rights of teachers and public workers. One milestone of this coalition was the staging of a large-scale rally in May 2006, when a reported 200,000 employees took to the streets protesting against a predominant practice of hiring on a contractual basis instead of formal recruitment through the Civil Service Board, which entitled employees to benefit from social protection and health-security schemes.[6] Before 2011, public-sector leagues were acting separately when seeking a new public salary scale. Following several overlaps in strike action and demonstrations for a new public-sector salary scale, the League of primary public school teachers invited the League of secondary public school teachers to act together under the UCC, which later on was joined by the remaining public-sector leagues and the private-sector teachers' union. According to Hanna Gharib, then president of the League of secondary public school teachers, the actions of the League of primary public school teachers were confusing and strange at the beginning of 2011. The primary public school teachers would call for a strike *exactly* one day before the secondary league would call for a strike. 'It felt like an act of sabotage to the effectiveness of our mobilisation. Our league would call for the boycott of official exam marking. The next day the primary league would call for a boycott of exam supervision. This was affecting our mobilisation. After these overlaps, the primary school teachers invited us to act together. I then understood that it was a way to put pressure on us to accept their invitation because our league was more powerful and they wanted to work with us to secure their demands. Even though I felt that a common mobilisation might create difficulties and complications, I accepted it.'[7] The leagues joined forces under the UCC in May 2012 in a 'gentleman's agreement', expressing their demands for a wage increase and a new salary scale for civil servants and public and private school teachers. The UCC became a coalition of the leagues of public primary and secondary school teachers, technical and vocational teachers, private school teachers and public-sector employees. The media referred to Hanna Gharib as the head of the UCC, although the committee did not plan to name a president.[8] Gharib became *ipso facto* leader of the UCC because the League of secondary public school teachers was the oldest and most active league among the UCC partners.[9] Hanna Gharib was by far the most charismatic president of the leagues under the UCC. He was born in 1953 in Tripoli in North Lebanon and lived in Akkar, one of the most disadvantaged regions in Lebanon. He participated in teachers' demonstrations and strikes from the 1970s onwards. He joined the Union of Lebanese Democratic Youth, which had close ties with the LCP, and became a member of the latter in 1972. He studied chemistry at the Lebanese University and became a public school chemistry teacher in 1981, with his first teaching assignment at the Zahiya Salman School in the Bir Hassan neighbourhood of Beirut. He was elected a representative of his school at a teachers' regional committee and was put in charge of the 'organisation of teachers' at the LCP. At the end of the war, Gharib was the secretary of the High Communication Committee of Secondary Teachers for West Beirut, Bekaa, North and South. At the same time, an executive committee for secondary teachers operated in another area covering East Beirut to Byblos. At the end of the war, he worked for several years to merge the two committees into one league, which was eventually created in 1991, and he was elected president of the League of secondary public school teachers in 2010.[10] He was defeated in the 2015 league elections before becoming secretary-general of the LCP in April 2016.

Difficulties and constraints of mobilisation

While the private-sector trade unions were acting on a vulnerable platform, public-sector employees were even more restricted than private-sector workers. In 1993, the graduates of the Administration Institute[11] were organised into one league, which became the League of public employees in 2012. This was a first in the history of civil servants (excluding public-sector teachers) in Lebanon. In 1959, civil servants were forbidden from engaging in political affairs, joining a political party or participating in strikes.[12] Law No. 144 issued on 6 May 1992 allowed civil servants to join political parties but continued to prohibit their association with any trade union. According to Article 65 of Law-Decree No. 112 from 1959, a civil servant's participation in a strike is akin to a resignation, which clearly violates freedom of association. Furthermore, Law-Decree 112 regulates the work of civil servants and does not differentiate between administrative staff and educational personnel, even though the latter do not perform any administrative, military or judiciary tasks and therefore could be granted additional rights, such as the right of association.

Although public-sector teachers are considered public employees, they are governed by an additional set of regulations. First, Decision No. 335 from 1972 gave primary educational staff the right to organise under 'cultural' leagues and made no reference to workers' associations or trade unions. Nevertheless, teachers transformed their leagues into a platform for demands in order to improve their working conditions as well as the quality of public education. In fact, Article 14 of Law-Decree No. 112 distinctly prohibited strikes and allowed for annulling the league plus new elections if strike action was pursued. The government did make use of this article of the law in 1973 when it expelled 300 primary teachers following their participation in a strike. Subsequently, Decision No. 335 was revoked in 1973 but was re-enacted in 1975.

Secondly, Article 16 considered the minister of education as the honorary president of primary school teachers' leagues, hence the minister acquired the contradictory roles of both minister and unionist. This article inhibited the independence of leagues and their autonomous decision-making. Thirdly, the main problem with Decision No. 335, promulgated under minister Najib abu Haydar, was that it instructed the creation of leagues for every governorate instead of one single national league that included all public primary school teachers in Lebanon. The separation of primary teachers into five regional leagues spawned additional divisions in the ranks of educational staff and had negative consequences for the decision-making process.[13] In 2010–11, the five regional leagues of the public primary schools united into one national league. This move strengthened the mobilisation of primary educational staff alongside their colleagues teaching in secondary schools, especially with regard to demands for a new salary scale the same year. Decision No. 871 dated 25 October 1980 gave secondary teachers the right to establish cultural, social and educational leagues, but this formulation was vague. The minister of education could stop the work of a league if its actions were deemed not to be in line with teachers' and public interests.

In turn, teachers considered that 'public interest' encompassed issues concerning 'public education' and 'salary improvement' and resorted to strikes as a tool to exert pressure. In 1980, Decision No. 871 gave secondary teachers the right to establish a cultural, social and educational league. Decision No. 871 stipulated the creation of one national league for all secondary public school teachers. This was not because of pressure exerted by teachers but rather due to the collapse of state institutions during the war. In fact, in the 1980s the state had lost its control over its different regions and educational institutions to militia control and authority. This was reflected in the provisions of Decision No. 871, which did not include significant restrictions compared to Decision No. 335 that was announced before the outbreak of the civil war.[14] While Decision No. 871 did not reiterate the strike ban, the Law-Decree No. 112 that regulates all civil servants including teachers still barred strike participation. However, throughout the years, secondary school teachers managed to bypass the prohibition and strikes, protests, negotiations and bargaining have become a seminal feature of the history of the mobilisation of secondary teachers, despite the legal restrictions.

In addition to constraints on public teachers' leagues, the Trade union of private-sector teachers, which made up a large segment of the UCC, was subject to strict regulations. Teachers, whether in the public or private sector, were subject to the same laws regulating wages, which explains why private teachers have acted together with public school teachers. Private school teachers and staff follow Law No. 5 governing private school teachers issued on 15 June 1956. This law specifies the legislative association between the private and public sector, mainly laws regulating wages and wage adjustment. Therefore, private- and public school teachers found themselves to be natural allies in their demands. However, private school teachers were governed by additional separate laws, which rendered the unionisation of teachers a risky decision due to dismissal regulations. Law No. 5 was subject to several reforms that made changes to recruitment conditions, salaries, benefits and working hours. The Union of private-sector teachers was linked to the Ministry of Labour. According to Article 100 of the Labour Code, it would come under the tutelage of the ministry should the union fail to set a date for board elections. At the same time, private-sector teachers came under the authority of the Ministry of Education and Higher Education (MEHE) when it came to issues concerning education and related matters. This dual set-up, under the Ministry of Labour and MEHE legislation, created ambiguity and instability. Examining the articles in the legislation concerning dismissal allows for a better understanding of the behaviour of private school teachers vis-à-vis public school teachers, as well as their relationship with school management, owners and their unions. Despite several amendments and reforms, the Lebanese law governing teachers in the private school sector had always included clauses relating to dismissal that continuously weakened the organisation and mobilisation of private-sector teachers. Private schools resorted to such provisions to discourage and dispirit teachers from joining unions. More precisely, the 1956 Law governing private-sector teachers provided several grounds for dismissal – legal dismissal (Article 31), punitive dismissal (Article 26) and arbitrary dismissal (Article 29). Article 12 granted schools the right to dismiss a teacher after two years of service. Article 26 allowed for dismissal in cases of immoral behaviour and neglect of duties. Furthermore, Article 29 gave schools the right to dismiss a teacher prior to 5 July, which marks the end of the school year. This article was considered a constant menace to teachers, especially for those planning to join a union. Several attempts to amend or revoke this article through the organisation of numerous protests were faced with an uncompromising rejection by schools, mainly religious schools, that constituted the bulk of private-sector educational institutions. Article 31 gave schools the right to dismiss a teacher should they contract an illness that would have a negative impact on their ability to teach. Article 38 stated that teachers subject to punitive dismissal were not entitled to any compensation. Together, these articles formed a major impediment to the unionisation of teachers, who feared dismissal because their employers disapproved of union members and their mobilisations and demands. Finally, the union membership of private-sector teachers was not compulsory, as opposed to public-sector teachers, who were required to be members of their respective leagues. This was a major difference – unlike their public-sector colleagues, private-sector teachers acted on a risky platform with a constant threat of dismissal. The fact that public school teachers and public employees were legally protected from arbitrary dismissal awarded them considerable strength in their mobilisation under the umbrella of the UCC. In this context, public-sector employees became more united while the private-sector GCWL suffered from serious internal divisions by the end of the 1990s, as shown in the previous chapter. In 1993, the League of public employees was created and the League of secondary public school teachers ended its internal rift and united again in 1995. Then in 2011, the five leagues of primary school teachers came together into one national league. What were the structural characteristics of the UCC that underpinned its survival and successful mobilisation?

Structural resilience

The structure of the leagues and the UCC can shed light on the resilience of its mobilisation in the face of state intervention and repression. The resilience of the UCC stemmed from its structural and institutional strength. First, the public sector employs around 30 per cent of the total wage earners in Lebanon.[15] In 2012, the UCC represented more than 200,000 workers and retirees, including 15,554 public servants,[16] 92,900 public and private teachers[17] and 82,300 public-sector retirees.[18] This large group of workers was mobilised against a single party – the state – and was able to act as a significant and unified pressure group. Second, the unity of public-sector workers and teachers was strengthened by the fact that there was only one league for public employees, one league for secondary teachers and one league for primary teachers. And it is legally prohibited to create other leagues to represent these employees.[19] Unlike the private sector, where more than one union could be established for the same group of workers, the fact that only one league could be created for teachers per educational level (primary and secondary) strengthened the weight and position of the teachers' leagues.[20] This allowed a higher level of representation compared to trade unions in the private sector.[21] Third, unlike private-sector union members, all public teachers and civil servants automatically became members of their leagues. This guaranteed a high representation of employees and therefore decisions taken by the executive board were more representative and hence legitimate.

Fourth, elections in the secondary teachers' league, the backbone of the UCC, were consistent and took place every two years and within the electoral deadlines. Rarely were these elections postponed or cancelled. These periodic elections gave the league legitimacy and representation that allowed it to resist political interventions. Around 6,000 secondary teachers distributed across 300 public schools elected their representatives – every 10 teachers elected 1 representative, with a maximum of 3 representatives per school. The representatives met at the national level to elect the administrative committee. In turn, the elected administrative committee would call the elected representatives to also elect the league's regional branches (at the governorate level). Around 550 elected representatives elected 18 members for the executive board: 6 members of the board had to represent the 6 Lebanese governorates, while the remaining 12 members obtained a seat on the executive board by securing the most votes, as there was no sectarian allocation of seats. That the League of secondary public school teachers' elections took place at the national level with Lebanon counting as one single district had the effect of flattening sectarian divisions. Also, the fact that the seats on the executive board were not allotted based on a sectarian formula stood in stark contrast to the prevalent forms of electoral practices in Lebanon. The sectarian affiliation of league members was irrelevant, which made their representation fair and based on their views and previous decisions on the issues rather than on sectarian calculations. Fifth, all the decisions of the UCC had to be reached by consensus. Each of the presidents of the leagues rallying under the UCC had the right to veto any proposed action. However, the right to veto was not used during the salary-scale mobilisation.[22] For instance, if the president of the League of public secondary teachers was against the call or strike, the UCC could not take the decision to go on strike. Each league's president in the UCC had to call for a general assembly at every school to give members the opportunity to vote for or against decisions regarding strikes and boycotts. The votes for and against strike action were counted and a strike was only called if the majority backed it. This was a lengthy process and could sometimes take two to three weeks. For instance, the open-ended strike called for by the secondary league in 2012 was approved by 95 per cent of representatives' votes. The vote in the general assembly gave actions legitimacy, protected the UCC from political pressure and guaranteed the unity of the UCC. Therefore, the democratic and independent decision-making of the UCC stemmed from the structure and internal regulations of its member leagues. This was a well-established process and mechanism in the UCC, even though no formal text existed that set out and regulated how it functioned. Finally, two leaders of the leagues under the UCC were long-term activists who had been at the forefront of the teachers' struggle. Hanna Gharib and Ni'mi Mahfud, the president of the Union of private-sector teachers, were both members of the LCP and had participated in the mobilisation of teachers since 1970. According to Hanna Gharib, 'the internal regulations of the secondary league that overlook sectarian affiliations are due to the role of the leftist secondary teachers who played a key role in drafting the internal regulation of their league, which organised administrative procedures for position assignment, as well as the electoral process without taking into account sectarian identities'.[23]

United for a new public-sector salary scale

Armed with a strong structure and large-scale mobilisation, the UCC launched its struggle for a new salary scale. The GCWL had planned a general strike to take place on 12 October 2011, expressing the workers' demands for a wage increase. Minister of Labour Charbel Nahas had already prepared a set of recommendations for the wage increase, based on the suggestions of the PIC. However, one day prior to the planned strike, the GCWL leadership entered into negotiations with the Government, subsequently took a stand-alone decision to cancel the strike and instead reached a settlement with the Government.[24] Many trade unions did not see themselves represented by the GCWL, and thus rejected the agreement, as the wage increase in the settlement was deemed insufficient. Mainly, the wage increase excluded those who earned more than LBP 1.8 million (US$1,200), which left a large proportion of wage earners without a wage increase. Some critics also declared that a wage increase alone was not enough and that improvements to the NSSF were necessary. As previously mentioned, the GCWL's position had drastically weakened after the war, and it continued to suffer from poor representation, while its leadership was under the umbrella of the Amal Movement. In fact, the head of the Amal Movement and Speaker of Parliament Nabih Birri participated in and heavily influenced the negotiations between the confederation and the Government.[25] The League of public employees and the Trade union of private school teachers, which were not part of the GCWL, but had taken part in the mobilisation, carried on their fight for a new salary scale without the GCWL and instead organised under the UCC.

The UCC's main demands comprised a wage increase of 121 per cent, which corresponded to the rate of inflation since 1996; the preservation of the historical fixed difference in the wages of university professors and secondary school teachers (a difference of six steps in the salary scale);[26] and a 60 per cent salary rise compared to primary education teachers, a right acquired 48 years earlier.[27] After the rise in wages for university professors negotiated in 2011, the salary gap between secondary school teachers and university professors drastically increased. While historically only 6 steps separated their wages, the gap had increased to 52 steps since the university professors' wage increase. For example in 2012, after 35 years of teaching, a university professor's wage stood at LBP 8.2 million (US$5,467) as opposed to LBP 3.2 million (US$2,133) for a secondary school teacher.[28]

After more than 48 days' strike, of which 33 days were continuous, 150 demonstrations and gatherings, 2 public exam boycotts,[29] and 3 large demonstrations of a magnitude that Lebanon had not witnessed since the 1970s, on 21 March 2013 the cabinet of Prime Minister Miqati approved the proposal for the increase in the minimum wage, the provision for cost of living and the amendment of basic salaries based on the new scale in the public sector. The UCC considered this a victory, as the Government was not able to stop the UCC actions, nor weaken or affect its unity.[30]

On 22 March 2013, only one day after submitting the law to Parliament, the Miqati cabinet resigned. Tammam Salam was appointed prime minister on 6 April 2013 and he formed a new cabinet ten months later in February 2014. Meanwhile, the proposed law on the new salary scale was submitted to Parliament in June 2013. For sixteen months, different parliamentary committees studied the salary scale and several amendments were made to the initial draft law. A special parliamentary committee that included members from the March 14 and the FPM, part of the March 8 coalition, finalised the last version of the draft law. The committee was boycotted by Hezbollah and the Amal Movement. The committee drastically amended the draft law in a way that mainly disadvantaged civil servants by justifying the increase in value-added tax, extending the working hours of civil servants, waiving the unity of legislation for private and public school teachers as per the 1956 Law governing private school teachers, and so on. Once the parliamentary committee had approved the draft law on 14 April 2014, the UCC called for a one-week strike in the public sector to protest against the amended law, culminating in a large demonstration on 14 May 2014, the day when the project law was to be enacted by Parliament. More than 100,000 people turned out for the scheduled demonstration, making it one of the largest popular actions of the UCC mobilisation. At the same time that the massive demonstration was taking place, the draft law was presented to Parliament's general assembly and only some of the articles were passed before the session was adjourned.

After the presidential vacuum that began on 25 May, three parliamentary sessions dedicated to the discussion of the draft law were adjourned due to the lack of a quorum. March 14 boycotted all three sessions, requesting a prior agreement on the salary-scale numbers and tax receipts before actually attending the parliamentary sessions.[31] Meanwhile, the March 8 coalition was boycotting parliamentary sessions convened to elect a president of the republic and to request prior agreement on a presidential candidate. Amid the tug-of-war between the March 8 and March 14 coalitions, public-sector workers were paying the price for the institutional paralysis and an unenforced new salary scale. In opposition to the draft law, the UCC declared a boycott of the drafting of marking standards, supervision and marking of the official exams taking place the following month.

With this action, the official exams were postponed for one week, allowing time for a parliamentary session to discuss the salary-scale legislation on 19 June 2014. However, a quorum could not be secured as the deputies continued to boycott all sessions. At that point, the Minister of Education and Higher Education Elias bu Sa'ab exerted pressure on the UCC by assigning the supervision of exams to alternative supervisors, such as retired teachers and administrative staff. Teachers firmly backed the UCC decision, despite the pressure exerted by political parties to break the boycott. The minister of education sought an arrangement with the UCC where teachers would supervise the exams, and in return would not be pressured to grade the papers unless the salary scale was announced by the time the official exams were taken. Indeed, after the official exams had taken place, the UCC suspended marking, as agreed with the minister of education.[32] Nevertheless, the minister exerted pressure on the UCC to start marking using the influence that political parties could exert over teachers.

He gathered together the UCC and members of the educational bureaus belonging to political parties – a majority of whom eventually voted for the marking of public exams[33] – and published statements pleading for teachers to break the boycott. Unexpectedly, the bureaus of the Amal Movement and the Future Movement retreated and issued opposing statements defying the orders of their leadership. This bold step encouraged the general assemblies of teachers' leagues to vote unanimously to uphold the marking boycott. The teachers' defiance of their political parties' position was a breakthrough in the sectarian political system and highlighted the strong, democratic and independent decision-making of the UCC. This was in stark contrast to the GCWL's lack of democratic decision-making and significant political intervention within its executive board, as explained previously. With this deadlock, the minister of education obtained cabinet approval to mark the exams without the participation of the public school teachers, and should that fail, certificates (i.e. baccalaureates) would be issued to all candidates. Once again, the teachers backed and upheld the UCC boycott and the minister of education was only able to mobilise forty-eight graders, half of whom were retired teachers. Facing strong and united teachers who were backing the UCC decision, the cabinet directed the minister to issue certificates to all exam candidates. Not one minister in the Salam cabinet opposed this decision. This revealed a consensus among all the political parties against the new salary scale for the public sector.[34]

Teachers were stripped of their most important pressure tool and strike action – the marking of official exams – which had been used many times before and had allowed them to win several wage-increase battles. This could be seen as the beginning of the end of the teachers' union movement. The political oligarchy was united in its action to weaken the UCC and resorted to sectarian affiliation and political intervention to defeat the mobilisation of public servants and teachers. However, while it was not able to achieve a new salary scale, the UCC remained united and independent despite the political consensus against its demands. The UCC may have been the only remaining platform for voicing socio-economic rights and demands in a climate where the deteriorating socio-economic situation of Lebanon's population was continuously overlooked. The UCC could not, however, continue to be impervious to political interventions and sectarian affiliations when operating within a heavily sectarian political system and a dormant labour movement. The importance of the non-sectarian character of the league was demonstrated by the latest attempt by the political establishment to co-opt the League of secondary public teachers by introducing sectarian politics into its governing body.

In the most recent elections of the board of the League of secondary public school teachers that took place on 25 January 2015, ten major political parties[35] joined forces under the Union Consensus List against the independent list formed by Hanna Gharib, then president of the league and a major driving force behind UCC mobilisation. The alliance of political parties agreed to nominate Abdo Khater, representing the Free Patriotic Movement (FPM), as their candidate running for the presidency of the League of secondary public school teachers. The Union Consensus list was composed of 17 candidates, leaving the eighteenth seat for Gharib as 'he is of an incontestable value to the league'.[36] Later, Minister of Education Elias bu Sa'ab declared that 'he made sure to secure seats for Hanna Gharib and another member of his list on the new league's board'.[37] However, some political parties instructed their delegates to vote for the entire list of seventeen without the addition of Hanna Gharib, fearing a large breakthrough. Representatives of some political parties declared, however, that leaving the eighteenth seat undefined was a deliberate move intended to provide the freedom for teachers' representatives to vote for the candidate of their choice.

The list of the coalition of political parties secured 16 out of 18 seats, while Hanna Gharib and another member on his list, Faysal Zayyud, won the two remaining ones. Gharib was on 60 per cent of the ballots, while his list gathered 40 per cent of votes.[38] More precisely, Hanna Gharib (299 votes) came third in the overall voting with only three votes separating him from the front runner, Abdo Khater (302), which shows the popularity of Gharib despite the smear campaign against him that blamed him for failing to secure the new salary scale. Abdo Khater was elected president of the league.[39] The scope and strength of the large political alliance against the coalition of independent teachers turned the elections into a reflection of political conflicts and tensions. Despite this interference, a large number of teachers remained independent and did not succumb to political intervention, as is evident from the election results. The fact that this political coalition included almost all political parties in Lebanon suggests that the sectarian cartel of the elite remained a serious threat to the emergence of an independent union movement. It was the organisational structure of the League of secondary public school teachers and its regulatory framework, both of which guaranteed democratic decision-making and representation, that had made union action possible and sustainable.

In February 2015, Hanna Gharib launched the Independent Union Movement (IUM) initiative in order to continue the battle for better working conditions and rights of teachers from within the league and from outside this platform. The IUM was not an alternative to the league but a movement operating within it aiming to build stronger mobilisation – it was the only tool left in its repertoire against the Government to achieve teachers' demands. In 2015, the IUM submitted to the league a proposal for a proportional electoral system within the league.

Following the new election of the board in January 2015, the UCC lost its foundation for successful mobilisation against the Government as the board had been co-opted by ten political parties that were mostly members of the Government at the time. In fact, on 20 February 2015, the UCC announced a press conference for 26 February and a strike call for 5 March without consultation with or prior knowledge of the League of secondary public school teachers. Both the conference and the strike were later called off, which closely resembled the behaviour of the GCWL, as seen in the previous chapter. The strike aimed to exert pressure on the parliamentary committee to meet and discuss the salary scale. Lacking pressure by the UCC, the parliamentary committee meeting achieved no result on 17 March. Consequently, on 26 March, the UCC admitted its failure vis-à-vis the ruling elite and called for another strike and protest outside the MEHE and in different regions. However, the protests did not attract large crowds. The UCC was receiving intervention and was under direct pressure from political parties. However, the administrative council of the league retreated and declared the academic year and the official exams a red line not to be crossed. Instead, the UCC called for a strike to take place on 23 April while waiting for the parliamentary committee to finalise the salary-scale draft legislation and to include it on the agenda of the first parliamentary session. Once again, the strike and the protest had a poor turnout. Meanwhile, the parliamentary committee did not meet. Subsequently, one day before the planned strike on 5 May, the UCC informed the Maronite Patriarch that the strike and protest had been called off. The UCC did not take part in the mobilisation against the waste crisis during the summer of 2015, but the IUM participated in the protests against the Government's handling of the waste problem. Meanwhile, the League of secondary teachers remained inactive, stating that the mobilising forces behind the protests were unknown. This position, as opposed to the previous league's resolute direction and decisions, placed the teachers outside an important mobilisation alongside the GCWL.[40] On 19 August 2015, the UCC organised a union conference and called for a strike for 9 September in order to exert pressure on the Government to take action. As had by now become routine practice, the strike was cancelled. The following month, on 30 September, the UCC called for a general strike to be staged on 20–26 October and to start again on 4 November to take place in parallel with the opening session of Parliament. The secondary league took part in all UCC's declarations and statements until this last recommendation, which created a rift between the two. The League of secondary public school teachers decided to organise a stand-alone strike on 20 October. However, this strike did not turn into an escalating mobilisation for the secondary league and was tamed by the loyalist political parties. On 3 November 2015, the league again participated in a strike organised by the UCC without having agreed to the demands with the other members of the UCC. Participation in the protest was once again low, which exposed the disagreement between the UCC representatives to the press. As a result of the weak UCC mobilisation, the draft salary-scale proposals did not appear on the agenda of the legislative session. It marked another failed opportunity for public-sector workers.

On the same day, the League of secondary public school teachers cancelled the planned strike scheduled for the following day. It also cancelled its plan to announce that the league was to become a union. This was despite the fact that the general assembly had recommended that both measures be taken. Furthermore, having previously threatened to boycott official exam marking, the league rescinded its decision. The IUM teachers were the only ones to show up at the marking centre to bring attention to their boycott. At this point, the mobilisation of public-sector workers faded and the UCC was considerably weakened. Still, the outbreak of a new wave of demonstrations suddenly followed, set in motion by the waste-management problem.

Towards the end of the three-year mobilisation, the UCC repeatedly declared its aspiration to become a federation with a formal union structure. This would have allowed it to take action in a more organised way and with a larger scope – taking campaigns beyond wage-increase and salary-scale demands. The UCC was sometimes accused of being wage-centric and lacking in support for other overarching national demands. Some have accused the UCC of being short of an overall long-term vision and being singularly focused on specific demands that do not concern a larger part of the population. This implies that a union structure might have allowed the UCC to move towards a larger scope of action, where it could support other unions and other workers' demands. A shift towards a union structure was seen by some to be a platform for a potential labour movement, given the paralysis of the GCWL.

Others perceived the UCC to be too large to be successful. According to Hanna Gharib, secondary teachers were discouraged and ultimately regretted the coalition with other leagues. In the past, as in 2008, secondary teachers had acted independently and had been able to have their demands met. Conversely, the coalition under the UCC involved larger demands, with a wage bill that weighed more heavily on the public budget, causing a forceful push back from the Government. In an interview with Gharib immediately before the 2015 elections, he stated that he sometimes perceived the collation of all the leagues under the UCC as a 'trap' orchestrated by the ruling elite. Gharib explained: 'In the past, we had managed to achieve our demands in stand-alone action. The fact that the League of secondary school teachers teamed up with the other leagues magnified the demands and therefore the pressure on the state. The large-scale demands and mobilisation pushed the Government to act violently against us. This might be one of the reasons behind our failure to achieve a new public salary scale.' When asked if bad intentions were meant by the League of primary public school teachers, Gharib said: 'At the beginning of 2012, the League of primary public school teachers organised its elections. The list backed by the Amal Movement won over the list backed by the LCP, to which I belong, Hezbollah and the FPM. I am not sure the Amal Movement is fond of me. Nevertheless, I decided to accept their offer to work all together.'[41]

On another level, the three-year mobilisation of the UCC proved that a good structure and regulations that guarantee democratic decision-making and representation make union actions possible and sustainable. It demonstrated that labour movements in Lebanon could exist. Reforms of the GCWL, its organisational structure and internal regulations along similar lines could lead to a revitalisation and independence from political intervention, thereby setting the stage for a new and more hopeful era for the workers' struggle in Lebanon.

In the end, a number of factors – the extended vacancy of the presidency of the republic, the delay in forming the cabinet, and the cancellation of parliamentary elections in 2013 – constituted a bottleneck that jammed the mobilisation of teachers and civil personnel at a time where any action towards change was needed. The restitution of the political system in Lebanon and the good functioning of its institutions remain the sine qua non condition for the revival of the labour movement in Lebanon. Again, Lebanon's political oligarchy played on political and sectarian affiliations so as to fragment and weaken a rising labour movement. However, the UCC showcased an active, present and united labour movement capable of rallying workers around their demands whilst lessening the dominance of sectarian affiliations within a profoundly sectarian system.

The relative silence of the UCC after the league elections in January 2015 was followed by demonstrations in response to the protracted waste crisis six months later. A group of civil society organisations were behind this four-month-long mobilisation, which rallied a share of the population irrespective of their sectarian identities and political affiliations. Similar to the mobilisation of public-sector employees, this movement – which expressed a social and political discontent of a group of citizens – was a cross-sectarian movement that focused on social demands.

The waste crisis and the mobilisation of civil society

A series of protests took place in July 2015 against the inability of the Government to solve a waste crisis. After the end of the civil war in 1990, the national waste management strategy mostly consisted of dumping waste from the central governorates of Beirut and Mount Lebanon into a single landfill site in the town of Na'ima south of Beirut. The waste-management contract was awarded to the private waste collector Sukleen. The Na'ima facility was opened in 1997 as a temporary landfill site to last for a period of ten years with a capacity of two million tons of waste. However, eighteen years later, the site had taken in an estimated 15 million tons of rubbish. While it was known several months in advance that Na'ima facility would shut down, the Lebanese Government designed no alternative strategy to deal with Lebanon's waste. This led to the Sukleen company to suspend its rubbish collections in July 2015 as it had run out of space at the dump site. This move caused waste to pile up around Beirut and Mount Lebanon, leading to the worst rubbish crisis in the history of Lebanon.

A series of small but growing protests began on 21 July and were led by a civil-society initiative called 'You Stink'. The dissent culminated in a pair of demonstrations that drew a few thousand people to the streets of Beirut in August. Protesters blamed the ruling elite for the lack of a long-term eco-friendly strategy to deal with solid waste in Lebanon. While protests first centred on the waste crisis, they eventually developed to focus attention on power cuts, political paralysis, political representation, corruption and government inefficiency. Protesters denounced the political leaders responsible for the waste crisis, setting aside sectarian identities and political affiliations. The importance of these protests was the emphasis on highlighting the state's failure to provide basic services and its overall poor performance.

The first demonstration gathered around a hundred protesters, mainly civil society activists, including environmentalists and feminists. The number of participants rose for the second protest on 28 July 2015, which secured more media coverage. Another large protest followed on 8 August, when three marches from different parts of Beirut converged at Martyrs' Square in the heart of Beirut. On 19 August 2015, protesters attempted to push away barbed wire that had been erected between them and government headquarters. The reaction of the police was violent – protesters were subjected to beatings, water cannons and arrests. The media coverage of the violence drew the attention of the public. At the next demonstration, the numbers of protesters surged. During this first wave of protests, demonstrations focused on the protracted waste problem and demanded the Government find a permanent and timely solution, without tackling wider political issues. Protesters were mainly civil society activists and political activists from left-wing parties.

The You Stink campaign and other civil society groups carried on with their actions and organised a protest on 22 August that brought together the largest gathering of protesters up to that point. Again, security forces intervened with excessive use of force, including water cannon and tear gas, and went as far as using live ammunition. A number of protesters were injured and others arrested. Protesters continued to arrive at Martyrs' Square on 23 August and clashes with security forces resumed. On 24 August, security forces pushed back protesters and installed cement walls to separate demonstrators from government headquarters.[42] On 25 August, security forces again resorted to force and arrested a number of protesters.[43]

On 28 August, the Civil Mobilisation, as it had come to be known, stated four key demands: the legal prosecution of all individuals found responsible for the shooting of protesters; the resignation of the minister of the environment due to his failure to manage the protracted waste crisis; the Government's release of tax receipts due to municipalities; and the organisation of parliamentary elections.[44] The Government was given 72 hours to meet the voiced demands. In addition to these four key points, the protest organisers declared in the same statement that 'the movement aims to establish a secular and democratic state and it will continue until it has secured all political and civil rights, a constant electrical power supply, the enactment of a new salary scale, guaranteed sovereignty of the judicial branch and freedoms including freedom of protest, justice to all social groups – notably those with special needs and the relatives of the war missing – in addition to ornganising municipal elections on time'. This statement redefined the mobilisation – from specific demands concerning Lebanon's waste crisis to a mobilisation with overarching political ones.

The demonstration following the 29 August statement was the largest of those organised by this movement. Thousands of protesters gathered in Beirut's two central squares; Martyrs' and Riyad al-Solh. The demonstration came to an end after a violent confrontation between protesters and security forces. Before the end of the 72-hour ultimatum, 30 protesters from the You Stink movement stormed the Ministry of Environment and began a sit-in on 1 September. The activists said that they intended to 'occupy the ministry until Minister Mohammad Machnuq stepped down'. Protesters were forced out of the ministry before the end of the day.[45]

The movement at this point had grown beyond addressing waste management and was voicing political demands concerning mainly transparency, accountability and the organisation of parliamentary elections. The movement was able to gather a heterogeneous group – people of different political affiliations, coming from diverse regions, came together to protest the failure of the state. This nascent cross-regional and cross-sectarian solidarity resembled the solidarity of the public-sector employees.

In addition to the frequent use of force, the ruling elite adopted the same tactics and lines of attack that it had employed to tame the UCC a few months earlier. The ruling elite united to manipulate sectarian identities in order to divide the protesters along pre-set sectarian alignments. One day after the 29 August demonstration, the Shiite Amal party organised a large-scale commemoration of its founder, Imam Mussa al-Sadr. This rally aimed to highlight the weight and popularity of the party following attacks voiced against its leader, President of Parliament Nabih Birri, during the waste-crisis protests. During the rally, Birri invited the political elite to convene national dialogue sessions to address the vacant presidency, the parliamentary electoral law and the government agenda. A few days later, on 4 September, the FPM, a part of the cabinet, organised a rally. Thousands of supporters of the Christian movement leader, Michel Aoun, descended on Martyrs' Square, calling for presidential elections and solutions to the political deadlock.[46] The next day, 5 September, the Christian Lebanese Forces party organised its annual mass in commemoration of its war martyrs. The party leader, Samir Geagea, pushed for electing a new president of the republic, which is the seat that belongs to the Christian community as set out in Lebanon's Constitution. On 10 September, Walid Junblat, the Druze leader of the PSP, received thousands of mourners in his mountain palace after a car bomb in Syria killed a prominent Druze cleric, Wahid al-Balus. The gathering was transformed into a popular event condemning the targeting of Druze sheikhs. This sectarian display and manipulation once again allowed the political elite to divert popular demands away from pressing political and socio-economic reforms, with extraordinary effectiveness. In fact, Lebanon remains mostly immune from wide-scale popular unrest.

In September and October 2015, a number of other protests were organised, but the movement had significantly weakened. On 8 October 2015, protesters took to the streets demanding that the cabinet urgently meet to organise waste collection without delay and find long-term solutions to the crisis. Despite the small number of protesters, security forces resorted to force, arresting a number of activists and bringing them before a military court. The 8 October protest was the last in the series of demonstrations relating to the waste crisis. From that date onwards, only a few small actions took place and the movement faded away as popular support had receded. On 11 March 2016, the cabinet approved a plan to establish two temporary landfills in Burj Hammud, east of Beirut, and in the coastal area of Costa Brava. It also agreed to reopen the Na'ima landfill site for two months – the closure of which eight months earlier had sparked the waste crisis. With this temporary patch-up solution, lacking any sustainable strategy, the protest was silenced.

Analysis of the three years of UCC mobilisation calling for a new public-sector salary scale reveals the resilience of public-sector workers despite several long-standing restrictions and the impact of sectarian affiliations on the functioning and performance of the UCC.

Public-sector workers were prohibited from organising in unions and participating in strikes. The Trade union of private-sector teachers was also subject to strict regulations such as legal provisions for dismissal, which were often used to discourage teachers from joining unions. Nevertheless, the three-year-long mobilisation revealed the structural and institutional strength of the UCC. The fact that public school teachers and public employees were legally protected from arbitrary dismissal was a considerable strength. Public-sector employees were able to act as a significant and unified pressure group, knowing that they constituted around 30 per cent of the total wage earners in Lebanon. Moreover, the fact that only one league could be created for civil servants and teachers for each educational level strengthened the weight and position of the leagues. Also, timely and regular elections in the leagues and the stipulation that all decisions had to be reached by consensus gave legitimacy to the UCC.

Against this backdrop, the teachers' defiance of their political parties' position, particularly when they opposed marking exams, was a breakthrough in the sectarian political system and highlighted the democratic and independent decision-making of the UCC. The attempt by the political establishment to co-opt the League of secondary public teachers by introducing sectarian politics into its governing body highlights the importance of the non-sectarian character of the movement and its challenge to the sectarian system. Following the co-optation of the UCC, which was the only platform for voicing socio-economic rights and demands, mobilisation during the 2015 waste crisis was similarly silenced through sectarian manipulation. The political elite successfully diverted popular demands away from pressing for political and socio-economic reforms.

The long-running mobilisation by the UCC proves that real representation and a democratic decision-making process make union actions possible and that labour movements in Lebanon can exist. The UCC demonstrated a united labour movement capable of rallying workers within a deeply entrenched sectarian system. It also showed that the way forward necessitated reform of the organisational structure and internal regulations of the GCWL to better support the workers' struggle in Lebanon.

Notes

1 Parts of this chapter were published in L. Bou Khater, 'Public sector mobilisation despite a dormant workers' movement', *Confluences Méditerranée*, 92:1 (2015), 125.

2 Lebanese Labour Watch, *al-Taqrir al-Sanawi al-Thalith: al-Ihtijajat al-ʿUmmaliyya fi Lubnan 2013* (Beirut: Lebanese Labour Watch, 2014), p. 11.

3 *Al-Akhbar English* (19 March 2013), p. 4.

4 *Al-Akhbar English* (26 February 2015), p. 6.

5 Hanna Gharib (2014), interviewed by Lea Bou Khater, 5 May. Hanna Gharib was president of the League of public secondary school teachers between 2010 and 2015.

6 In an attempt to reduce the budget, the Lebanese Government issued a decree in 1996 under which it stopped formal recruitment to the civil service. However, hiring continued on a contractual basis and formal recruitment resumed on a small scale in 2008.

7 *Ibid.*

8 According to Gharib, the members of the UCC did not agree on the media referring to him as president.

9 *Ibid.*

10 *As-Safir* (1 May 2013); *L'Hebdo* (10 May 2013).

11 A state agency for administrative reform.

12 According to Article 15 of Law-Decree No. 112 of 12 June 1959, civil servants are forbidden from taking part in political affairs, joining a political party or participating in strike action.

13 I. Samaha, *Jadaliyat al-Haraka wa al-Waʿi Bayna Afrad al-Hay'aa al-Taʿlimiyya fi Lubnan* (Beirut: Dar al-Farabi, 2006). Organisation within regional leagues affected the electoral process, and delay marked the elections of primary leagues. Elections in the different governorates would take several months and sometimes even an entire year due to the intervention of political parties and political elites, especially in peripheral areas. The electoral system in the primary league consisted of teachers voting for their representatives: every 10 teachers elect 1 representative with a maximum of 3 representatives per school. Elected representatives of every regional district (*Caza*) elect a district committee composed of 15 members. The committees then elect the governorate committee (1 league for each of the 5 governorates), which was actually the regional league. Elections in the secondary teachers' league were organised at the national level, which made political intervention more difficult.

14 *Ibid.*

15 The World Bank, *Lebanon – Good Jobs Needed.*

16 R. Azour, 'Personnel Cost in the Central Government. An Analytical Review of the Past Decade', Institut Des Finances Basil Fuleihan, p. 1, www.institutdesfinances.gov.lb (accessed 19 November 2017).

17 Distribution of teachers per sector and work status for the year 2012–13: 26,084 public school teachers, 14,308 contractual teachers in the public sector, 915

volunteers in the public sector, 31,681 private school teachers, 19,02 private school contractual teachers and 808 volunteers.

18 *Al-Akhbar* (25 April 2014), p. 8.

19 Decision No. 871 stipulated the creation of one national league for all secondary public school teachers. This is not due to pressure exerted by teachers but again to the collapse of state institutions during the war. In fact, in the 1980s, the state had lost its control over its different regions and educational institutions to militia control and authority. This is reflected in the provision of Decision No. 871, which lacked significant restrictions compared to Decision No. 335 promulgated before the outbreak of the civil war.

20 As per Decision No. 871 for the creation of the League of secondary public school teachers.

21 Hanna Gharib (2014), interview.

22 *Ibid.*

23 *Ibid.*

24 The minimum wage rose from LBP 500,000 (US$333) to LBP 700,000 (US$467). Those earning less than LBP 1 million (US$667) would receive an extra LBP 200,000 (US$133). Employees who earned between LBP 1 million (US$667) and LBP 1.8 million (US$1,200) would expect an increase of LBP 300,000 (US$200).

25 Friedrich-Ebert-Stiftung, *Period Review October 2011: Debate on Salary Increase Reveals Both the Trade Unions' Weakness and the Need for Large-scale Economic Reform* (Beirut: Friedrich-Ebert-Stiftung, 2011).

26 Azour, 'Personnel Cost in the Central Government', p. 5. Civil servants in Lebanon are classified in 5 grades. Each grade is composed of 22 steps, and each step determines the salary category. Every 2 years the civil employee moves up the ladder of steps. Teachers belong to grades 3 or 4, with each grade comprising 52 steps.

27 In 1966, the Government stipulated 5 additional hours on top of 15 teaching hours to cope with the shortage of secondary public school teachers. The extra hours were accompanied by an increase in salaries of 60 per cent.

28 Salary-scale comparison exercise prepared by Hanna Gharib, unpublished.

29 Lebanese Labour Watch, *al-Taqrir al-Sanawi al-Thalith: al-Ihtijajat al-'Ummaliyya fi Lubnan 2013* (Beirut: Lebanese Labour Watch, 2014).

30 Hanna Gharib (2014), interview.

31 On 25 May 2014, the term of President of the Republic Michel Suleiman ended without a successor. During the first parliamentary session dedicated to the presidential elections held on 23 April 2014, none of the candidates reached a two-thirds majority vote during the first round, and there was no quorum to hold the second round, which needed a simple majority of votes. Between 30 April 2014 and 28 September 2016, 45 rounds of elections failed because the quorum had not been met. It was only on 31 October 2016, following more than two years of presidential vacuum, that Michel Aoun was elected president of the republic.

32 Many demonstrations and sit-ins in front of several ministries were organised. Ali Berro, a Ministry of Agriculture employee, went on a 20-day hunger strike that he ended on 8 July 2014.

33 The educational bureaus of the Progressive Socialist Party, the FPM, the SSNP, the Future Movement, the Amal Movement, the Democratic Left, the Phalanges Party, the Lebanese Forces and the Democratic Party invited teachers to start exam marking. In opposition, parties such as the Communist Party and the People Movement were against teachers marking the exams.

34 Hanna Gharib (2014), Interview.

35 *Al-Akhbar* (26 January 2015). These parties included the Free Patriotic Movement, the Amal Movement, Hezbollah, the Lebanese Forces, the Future Movement, Marada and the PSP.

36 *Al-Liwa'* (15 July 2015), p. 9.

37 *Ibid.*

38 *Daily Star* (26 January 2015), p. 4.

39 The newly elected board of the league was composed of: 1. Abdo Khater (FPM, 302 votes); 2. Youssef Zaghlut (Hezbollah, 301 votes); 3. Hanna Gharib (LCP, 299 votes); 4. Nazih Jibawi (Amal Movement, 298 votes); 5. Marta Dahdah (Marada, 298 votes); 6. Ahmad Khayr (Future Movement, 297 votes); 7. Maher Mer'i (Progessive Socialist Party, 297 votes); 8. Ghada al-Za'tari (Future Movement, 295 votes); 9. Hiyam abi 'Abdallah (Free Patriotic Movement, 295 votes); 10. Ali Haydar (Hezbollah, 290 votes); 11. Essmat Daw (Socialist Party, 290 votes); 12. Barakat Taleb (Future Movement, 289 votes); 13. Jirji Nasr (SSNP, 289 votes); 14. 'Abdallah Najim (Lebanese Popular Conference, 289 votes); 15. Ja'far 'Assaf (Amal Movement, 285 votes); 16. 'Abd al-'Ali (Islamist Labour Movement, 285 votes); 17. Faysal Zayyud (Independent, 277 votes).

40 *Al-Akhbar* (9 September 2015), p. 6.

41 Hanna Gharib (2014), interview.

42 After continuous protests in Riyad al-Solh Square in front of the newly erected cement wall, the prime minister ordered its removal within 24 hours and cancelled the results of the waste-management services tender – a victory for protesters.

43 Meanwhile, the minister of the environment declared the results of the bidding process for the waste-management contract. The proposed waste-management strategy assigned a landfill site to each governorate or region to be managed by private waste collectors at higher rates than those charged by the previous collector, Sukleen.

44 Parliamentary elections had been suspended since 2013. Elections were declared postponed until May 2018.

45 This initiative was secretly organised by You Stink without any prior coordination with other organisations or campaigns taking part in the overall movement against the waste crisis. They had, in fact, gathered in a meeting to discuss the future steps to be taken. Following this meeting, all groups and organisations rallied under 'The Follow up Committee of August 29 protests'.

46 On 25 May 2014, the president's term ended without a successor being elected, leading to a political vacuum. Since 2014, all parliamentary sessions dedicated to presidential elections have failed to meet the required quorum due to the boycott by Hezbollah and the FPM MPs, who demanded an agreement to back one candidate prior to their participation in elections.

Conclusions and notes for future forms of labour power

The book explores the break-up of labour power in a small open economy coated with a thick layer of sectarianism. All told, the trials and tribulations of the labour movement in Lebanon reveal how the struggle of labour against capital deepens when taking place in a state governed by a sectarian power-sharing system. Labour organising is perceived as a potential vehicle for rebellion against the sectarian-liberal system of rule, which put the regime at odds with any ambitious attempts of labour organising with the aim of making effective social and economic demands. Instead of resorting to repression and persecution, the state co-opted the labour movement and distorted the confederation of unions into a mouthpiece for the ruling elite and bargaining tool in their feuds over the sectarian allocation of privileges and resources.

More significantly, the book examines how the liberal-sectarian system rests on the decomposition of labour power into a scattered and fragmented movement. The maintenance of the power-sharing system or the 'allotment state' used by the sectarian elites to capture economic benefits hinges on the ongoing co-optation and manipulation of the labour movement. Rather than sectarian identities and sectarianism, the story of the labour movement sheds light on a process of sectarianisation. If we seek to understand the durability of the sectarian political system in Lebanon, it is necessary to look into how state elites have curbed, co-opted, sectarianised and used the labour movement to preserve the sectarian 'allotment state' and halted any attempts to organise that override sectarian identities.

As organised labour emerged during the French mandate, which installed the logic and pillars of the Lebanese state and its elite, the labour movement was not built on pillars resilient enough to allow for growth and strength. The labour movement was influenced by the institutionalisation of sectarianism and the ideological concerns of political parties, whereby trade union federations were divided between those that collaborated with right-leaning political parties and trade unions that joined forces with those parties on the left. During the same period, elites moulded state institutions in accordance with their financial and commercial interests. Among the first policies adopted by the independent Lebanese state were the progressive deregulation of trade and exchange systems plus the stabilisation of the Lebanese pound. The adoption of such measures put industry and agriculture under severe pressure. The business-financial elite's capacity to shape public policy rose commensurately at the expense of labour rights and conditions.

To further protect the sectarian-liberal system of rule, the Lebanese state adopted restrictive regulations on the workforce and trade unions. Lebanon did not ratify the ILO Convention No. 87, Freedom of Association and Protection of the Right to Organise, because it clearly did not want to allow for the development of strong trade unions capable of challenging state policies and elite interests. In line with abstaining from ratifying the convention, the Labour Code promulgated in 1946 explicitly limited freedom of association. The code dealt with trade unions as threats to sectarian power-sharing. The legal provisions in the Labour Code gave a substantial role to the state in the controlling of employment conditions and the management of trade union affairs. The law also restricted the associations of public-sector employees. Civil servants and public school teachers were and still are prohibited from partaking in political affairs or participating in strikes. While the legislation was amended to allow civil servants to join political parties, it continued to prohibit their association with any trade union. From that, one might infer that labour organising is more threatening to Lebanon's ruling elite than political parties organised along sectarian lines. The restrictive legal provisions have been major obstacles to the flourishing of the labour movement, and they are still in place today.

In addition to legal constraints, the labour movement has, since its birth, been hampered by a problematic organisational structure. The GCWL charter promulgated in 1970 remained unchanged until 2020 despite being considered by many to obstruct the labour movement. The GCWL's structure was initially designed to reduce disagreements between opposing union federations affiliated to different political parties, but lacked two key democratic safeguards. First, the lower part of the organisational body did not elect the decision-makers at the top: the CR did not elect the executive council. Second, the confederation electoral system did not adhere to proportional representation: federations were awarded the same number of votes even though the size of federations varied significantly. This structure produced an undemocratic and unrepresentative organisation unfit to represent Lebanon's workers. And it set the confederation up for political intervention through electoral engineering. While there have been many attempts since the 1980s to reform the GCWL, the 1970 charter remains in force to this day – intentionally perpetuating the fragmentation and impotence of the labour movement and entrenching sectarian power-sharing.

During the civil war, the GCWL was unable to adopt a unified political vision and instead took vague positions due to the political divergence of its members, resulting in a tedious decision-making process. The post-war period witnessed state intervention on a larger scale; political intervention and pressure were used to guarantee the elections of loyalist trade unionists. And it was through the proliferation of member federations that the state succeeded in controlling the GCWL. The Syrian presence in Lebanon and its interference in Lebanese internal politics also played a significant role in reducing the influence and power of the labour movement. Furthermore, the prevalence of the tertiary sector, the small size of the majority of private-sector enterprises and the high levels of informality, together with low levels of industrialisation, spelled a structurally weak position of workers. In brief, capital enjoys the rents and benefits while labour is co-opted through sectarian patronage. The post-war era witnessed the private sector participating in electoral politics whereby the business-financial elites were closely wedded to political forces and united in one power elite. Beyond controlling the labour movement to circumvent a challenge to the overall system and ensure political stability, the GCWL was used as a tool in the disputes of the elites over power, rents and benefits.

In this manner, the political establishment co-opted the UCC as it force-fully led the three-year-long mobilisation for a new public-sector salary scale. The ruling elite adopted its tried-and-tested co-optation strategy – introducing sectarian politics into the UCC governing body. The mobilisation of the UCC underlined the importance of the non-sectarian character of the movement and its fundamental challenge to the established system. The experience of the UCC demonstrated that *real* representation and a democratic decision-making process make a united labour movement capable of rallying workers within a deeply entrenched sectarian-liberal system. It also underlined the urgent need to reform the GCWL's obsolete organisation, structure and regulations to revitalise a much-needed labour movement.

Following the co-optation of the UCC, the last large-scale labour mobilisation in Lebanon, the movement that emerged from the 2015 waste crisis was immediately silenced through the usual sectarian manipulation methods to curtail any challenge to the system and the elite's grip on the resources of the state.

The decomposition of labour power was secured in double measure by Lebanon's starved social protection in general, and social insurance in particular. The primary purpose of the Lebanese social protection policies was never to eliminate extreme poverty, reduce inequality or expand citizenship. Historically, social policy in Lebanon contributed to a dynamic of exclusion where the upper and middle classes of society were well served by a subsidised private sector. Compared to informal workers, these were a set of relatively privileged workers, although unequally and precariously provided for by the state in regards to health insurance, family allowances and end-of-service lump-sum payments. Aside from this assistance, unemployment benefit and insurance against disability and accidents at work are currently non-existent. Most informal workers, such as seasonal labourers, construction and agricultural workers, migrant and domestic workers, as well as the self-employed, unemployed and retirees, remain unprotected. Melani Cammett notes that 'sectarianism and the provision of social services entail the construction of boundaries of inclusion and exclusion, and through their welfare activities, identity-based organizations create or perpetuate group membership'.[1] For instance, the limited oversight of the state over private schools extends the authority of sectarian organisations and other non-state providers in education. Most Lebanese are educated by such organisations rather than public schools, which perpetuates the influence of sectarian leadership.

It is, then, not surprising that Lebanon is one of the few remaining countries in the world that lacks a national pension scheme, resulting in the perpetuation of clientelism along sectarian lines. In short, the NSSF, the central institution tasked with the protection of workers and their dependents, is marred with corruption, clientelism and lack of funds. Instead, workers and their families remain clients of their respective sectarian leaders and their non-state institutions when it comes to accessing basic services such as education and healthcare, plus any type of social assistance.[2] In a society where the public welfare system is underdeveloped, welfare can become the 'terrain of political contestation',[3] and as has happened in Lebanon, sectarian elites step in to provide basic social services. Hence, through the capture of the GCWL and the failing NSSF, the Lebanon sectarian elites also control the labour force through the traditional patron–client relationship. In a context where the state is hollowed out, the labour movement co-opted and social protection ignored by the state, workers are left without protection except for traditional sectarian patronage. The result is a thriving sectarian-liberal system. 'It is usually in countries where economic inequality has been addressed and a welfare state has been installed that sectarianism or ethnic mobilization has noticeably decreased because such interventions curb the power of clientelism and sectarian patronage.'[4] I asserted that breaking labour power is one of the tools used for making the institutionalisation of sectarianism robust. Therefore, I explored the constraints – the shackles – imposed by the sectarian system on the labour movement to make the obstructions strong and durable.

The link between sectarianisation and a weak labour movement may receive further confirmation from cases like Iraq. The Iraqi Government ratified Convention 98 on the Right to Organise and Collective Bargaining in 1962 and in June 2018 ratified Convention 87 on Freedom of Association and Protection of the Right to Organise. But following the US invasion, the Coalition Provision Authority, headed by Paul Bremer, retained Saddam Hussein's laws that aimed to curb collective bargaining and trade union activity, in turn maintaining the suppression of labour associational power, while liquidating Iraq's capital assets and resources.[5] According to Naomi Klein, Iraq was used to pilot extreme neoliberal principles after the US invasion in 2003.[6] Despite Iraq's ratification of Convention 98 from 1962, the Iraqi Government has refused to recognise unions and labour leaders and activists have been exiled, sacked and assassinated, and their offices attacked and destroyed. Iraqi workers have been organised in detrimental conditions with no legal or financial power. A long-standing demand for a new Labour Code that awards Iraqi workers legal protection was voiced by actors from across the labour movement until a new code was promulgated in 2015. Today, research on workers and trade unions in Iraq is scant. The 'institutionalization of sectarianism' in Iraq following the US invasion may explain why the literature on 'political sectarianism' receives most attention from scholars of Iraq. As opposed to social sectarianism, which has long been manifested in social traditions, celebrations, and so on, and has seldom been reflected politically, 'political sectarianism erodes notions of citizenship and nationalism, and reduces the state and society to a medley of exclusive sects struggling with each other for power (immaterial and real) and resources'.[7] This 'amplification of the sectarian logic'[8] had an effect on scholarship that, then, not unlike in Lebanon, largely overlooked other elements of Iraqi society, such as workers and labour movements.

Against traditional unionism and the state

What implications can this pattern of co-optation have for contentious politics and the future of the 2019 October Revolution? The co-optation of the labour movement during the post-war period explains the absence of labour power during the October Revolution and the limited impact of the uprising. The labour movement had been fully outflanked and was no longer capable of fighting for change and workers' rights. The co-optation of the labour movement commencing in the 1990s was organised for exactly this purpose: to maintain the system, perpetuate political stability and curtail any push for change.

In October 2020, one year since the start of the October Revolution, the streets were empty and the country seemed in a worse condition. The economic meltdown continues, short of an economic reform plan, while inflation, poverty and unemployment are soaring. On the first anniversary, the October Revolution had failed to dislodge the inept and corrupt political elite. The former Prime Minister Sa'ad Hariri, who resigned the previous year, was once again nominated to form a new cabinet. And more than two months later, the domestic investigation into the devastating explosion at Beirut's port has failed to yield any credible results.

The book redirects attention to the role of labour co-optation in diluting and weakening contentious politics and stifling change during social unrest following Lebanon's waste crisis in 2015 and the October Revolution. The decline of the labour movement not only threatens working conditions but also affects the quality, scope and action of civil society and political life in general. The weakening of the workers, who are the largest and most significant civil actors, hampers the potential and strength of society to challenge. In the absence of organised labour, the struggle for change is looking exceedingly arduous in the first year of the October Revolution.

Looking at the Middle East, Eva Bellin notes how 'labor's value as a political ally has only increased as slowed growth and economic austerity have undermined the popularity of so many MENA regimes'.[9] The GCWL did not take action to protect the laid-off employees or advocate for an urgent wage adjustment, as wages lost their value amid skyrocketing inflation. Nor did the confederation denounce the apathy of the Government vis-à-vis the soaring poverty, but, true to form, sought to curry favour with the elite by calling for the prompt formation of a government. The recently elected president of the confederation threatened to organise strikes and protests in the event that a new cabinet was not formed swiftly – a standpoint that simply echoed the position of the state elite and the Amal Movement in particular. In a staged non-competitive election in March 2017, Bishara al-Asmar was elected president of the GCWL, along with eleven members of the executive bureau.[10] Thanks to the multiplication of federations, the Amal Movement alone captured 48 members of the executive council and therefore controlled the decision-making. The Amal Movement is assumed to have selected Bishara al-Asmar, president of the Union of port employees, who in the past often sided with Nabih Berri against Rafiq Hariri in their 'allotment'-related feuds, especially regarding the control of the Port of Beirut.[11] In the next three years, the confederation is unlikely to make any gains and demands will be steered by the rising conflict between Nabih Berri and the President of the Republic Michel Aoun in their clashes over spoils.

In May 2019, al-Asmar was detained for ten days and forced to resign after making offensive remarks about the late Lebanese Maronite Patriarch Cardinal Nasrallah Boutros Sfeir. Al-Asmar was sitting on a panel and was overheard making degrading jokes about Patriarch Sfeir, unaware that he was being recorded. Some observers believe that the FPM leaked the video as part of their rivalry with the Amal Movement. After a year out of the public eye, al-Asmar was suddenly re-elected president of the confederation in July 2020 in the same non-competitive manner as three years earlier. This occurred at an important juncture of increasing tensions over economic reforms amid the economic meltdown, including the decision to waive state subsidies. The Lebanese Government had been subsidising a large number of goods and services, including wheat, fuel, drugs, medical services and education. The subsidy policies were expanded in 2020 to include basic food staples in order to mitigate the effects of the foreign-currency crisis and devaluation of the Lebanese pound, at an estimated total cost of US\$710 million per month.[12] Given the depletion of foreign reserves, subsidies would be expected to expire at best in early 2021. The GCWL was quick to oppose subsidy removal, staging a small protest in front of its headquarters. It echoed reassuring messages from political leaders and was working to calm down their constituencies despite the obvious lack of funds. Bellin posits that organised labour may be unassertive in safeguarding democratic and representative processes when it is the beneficiary of extensive state sponsorship – including financial subsidies and legal concessions, such as exclusive domains and closed-shop, profit-sharing schemes – privileged access to social welfare programmes and subsidised credit and urban housing.[13] In Lebanon, state sponsorship is replaced by sectarian patronage, which has wedded organised labour to the sectarian status quo, making it unreceptive to change inside and outside the confederation. It guarantees the GCWL's antipathy towards change – the confederation has remained steadfastly allied to the state elite despite the political stalemate and economic meltdown.

Today, traditional unionism based on mediation between workers and capital is often not able to defend the workforce it pledges to represent. According to some observers, 'traditional unions are part of the institutional setting to maintain capitalism'.[14] Typically, trade unions are beneficial to employers as they prefer to deal with a representative body and undermine workers' autonomy, and at the same time guarantee that workers will respect agreements. In recent years, traditional trade unions have not played an important role in social movements and have often simply joined the protests, riots and uprisings organised and led by other movements. With the intensification of privatisation, deregulation and reduction of public subsidies, unions are not up to the job and new forms of organised labour have emerged.[15] The surge of new forms of workers' organisations in both the Global South and Global North contests the view that the workers' struggle is no longer relevant and challenges the vision that the revival of traditional unionism is needed. However, little attention has been paid to these new forms of labour struggle which use innovative means of blockade, strike practices and occupation of workplaces. New forms of workers' organisations have even contributed to toppling the Government in Egypt and initiating an uprising in Bosnia.[16]

In Lebanon, it is crucial to keep an eye on new forms of collective action by organised workers emerging within and around social movements and their role in the uprising. As workers and professionals grapple with unemployment, salary cuts and lay-offs, as well as a three-digit rate of inflation and exchange-rate collapse while lacking any social protection, labour protests and organising seem to be resurfacing. An estimated 2,500 Civil Defence volunteers organised several sit-ins and protests in front of the Ministry of Interior demanding that the cabinet secure them paid, full-time jobs. Most are paramedics, rescue workers and firefighters. It is these volunteer firefighters, whom the state refused to acknowledge and protect, that were ordered to respond to the fire that led to the port explosion on 4 August 2020, with no warning of what was stored in Hangar 12. Nine firefighters and a paramedic were the first to perish in the blast. Innovative action has also come from other areas. Several times in 2020, cement-truck drivers took collective action and blocked main roads in North Lebanon in protest at delayed payment of wages and threats of mass lay-offs. In an attempt to assert more pressure, they used their six-wheel trucks to block off the northern entrance to Beirut.

The plight of migrant workers, stranded in Lebanon without any form of protection, has also worsened amid the economic crisis. Migrant workers, considered to be the most vulnerable category of workers legally, socially, economically and linguistically, have started to protest for the first time against salary cuts and lay-offs. In May 2019, 400 migrant cleaning workers from Bangladesh and India organised week-long strikes asking for one day off per week, payment in the first five days of the month, and for all abuse to stop. These workers are paid in Lebanese pounds, and since the devaluation of the currency their wages have fallen sharply. Sudanese workers also organised a continuous four-month sit-in outside their embassy in Beirut. The double economic and health crises compounded by the port explosion have led to many lay-offs. As they are mostly daily-wage earners, they have been left struggling for cash, unable to afford food and shelter. Most have entered Lebanon illegally and do not have the funds to purchase a ticket to return to their home country; they asked to negotiate their return home with both Lebanese and Sudanese authorities. Migrant domestic workers, mainly Ethiopian and Ghanaian nationals, who have also been facing harsh working conditions and felt the foreign currency shortage, have organised community assistance and a series of protests in front of their embassies in Beirut. A new standardised contract adopted in September 2020, aiming to improve the working conditions of around 250,000 domestic workers excluded from labour protection, was revoked by the State Shura Council less than two months later. It is the very first time that migrant workers have come together to protest against their difficult working conditions, and this is a huge step in itself that reveals the onset of a consciousness of their numbers and strength.

Other forces like the Lebanese Professionals Association (LPA) started organising in October 2019. A group of professionals began to mobilise under the umbrella of the newly formed LPA. Inspired by the Sudanese Professionals Association, various groups of professionals have used the impetus of the October protests to coordinate alternative labour movements. They quickly joined forces and together formed the LPA on 28 October 2019. The LPA declared its participation in the October uprising in protest against the political and economic system and calling for a democratic transition to a secular state based on social justice. Even though the LPA is composed of several associations – university professors, engineers, doctors, artists, journalists, media workers and workers in NGOs – it is still a nascent attempt at alternative organising. Briefly after its establishment, the LPA called for a march to start from GCWL headquarters towards Martyrs' Square in protest against the confederation's silence. 'We want unions that represent us', said the flyer calling for the march. This illustrates the need to configure new forms of workers' organisations that use strategies and set goals that differ from conventional unions.

As an emergent association, the LPA faces organisational challenges that still require lengthy discussion and probably new approaches to organising that supersede the traditional structures of trade unions or professional orders and sidestep the required Ministry of Labour pre-authorisation. A serious challenge is the structure of the LPA, which remains under debate. The current decision-making process is ambiguous and does not guarantee the representation of the different associations. These obstacles have already questioned the viability of the LPA as an umbrella body that can coordinate among the various members, set the political agenda of the movement and define positions vis-à-vis the new government and its policies. This umbrella organisation might need more time to acquire a representative structure and would be wise to raise questions concerning its internal regulations, decision-making process and outreach. Even if the LPA today is facing structural and organisational challenges, it has demonstrated the capacity to imagine and experiment with new forms of social organising.

The launch of the LPA stems from accumulative experiences and actions during previous years. Several founding members of the LPA were activists in previous popular protests and mobilisations from 2005, including the Cedar Revolution – the largest nationwide protests that successfully demanded the withdrawal of Syrian troops from Lebanon following the assassination of Prime Minister Rafiq Hariri. And some members of the Independent Professors Association were already campaigning within the public Lebanese University long before the 2019 Revolution. 'Our activism and our demands are not new. But the momentum of the October Revolution has put our demands at the forefront and brought us all together under the LPA', asserted Wafa Noun, a university professor and activist.[17] Other members have said how the 2015 mobilisation was a pivotal point in terms of the need for labour organising and overcoming the fear of traditional frameworks of representation.

A series of protests took place in July 2015 against the state's inability to devise a national waste-management strategy, leading to the worst waste crisis in the history of Lebanon. The movement grew beyond addressing the crisis and voiced political demands concerning transparency and accountability and the organisation of parliamentary elections. Most importantly, the movement was able to rally people of different political affiliations, from diverse regions, who came together to protest against the failing state. However, this nascent cross-regional and cross-sectarian solidarity was soon tamed by the ruling elite. The elites united in their manipulation of sectarian identities by staging rallies and events to divert popular demands away from pressing political and socio-economic reforms. The movement faded away. At this juncture, activists who were interviewed attested to the limited power and capability of structure-less and leaderless movements to challenge the ruling elite. It has brought to the fore the need for an organisation and structure that can sustain a long-term struggle and guarantee coordination across the country when countering the moves of the ruling elite.

Retelling the story of the labour movement in Lebanon is not about the downfall and defeat of labour. On the contrary, the history of traditional unionism reveals the fear and trepidation of the sectarian liberal system. The state elite's continuous attempts to undermine the labour movement are evidence that a resilient and vigorous labour movement constitutes an all-important threat to the political system in place. The decline of the organised labour movement does not imply that class struggle is no longer relevant. Rather, it means that capital and the state until now have been winning this struggle. While it faces enormous hurdles, contemporary forms of workers' struggles that appeal to class solidarity and show a different kind of unionism can provide an alternative vision and counteract the Lebanese sectarian-liberal system.

Notes

1 M. Cammett, *Compassionate Communalism: Welfare and Sectarianism in Lebanon* (Ithaca, NY: Cornell University Press, 2014), p. 217.
2 R. Leenders, *Spoils of Truce: Corruption and State-Building in Postwar Lebanon* (Ithaca, NY: Cornell University Press, 2012), p. 153.
3 Cammett, *Compassionate Communalism*, p. 5.
4 R. Majed, 'Sectarianization: mapping the new politics of the Middle East', *Global Change, Peace, & Security*, 31:1 (2018), 121–4.
5 T. Ismael, J. Ismael and G. Perry, *Government and Politics of the Contemporary Middle East: Continuity and Change* (Abingdon: Routledge, 2016), p. 253.
6 N. Klein, 'Baghdad Year Zero: Pillaging Iraq in Pursuit of Neocon Utopia', *Harpers*, 309:1852 (2004), p. 44.
7 T. Ismael and J. Ismael, *Iraq in the Twenty-First Century: Regime Change and the Making of a Failed State* (Abingdon: Routledge, 2015) pp. 78–9.
8 *Ibid.*, p. 103.
9 E. Bellin, *Stalled Democracy: Capital, Labor, and the Paradox of State-Sponsored Development* (Ithaca, NY: Cornell University Press, 2002), p. 181.
10 77 out of the 80 members making up the executive council which participated in the elections voted for al-Asmar.
11 Leenders, *Spoils of Truce*, pp. 188–95.
12 *Al-Akhbar* (21 September 2020), p. 11.
13 Bellin, *Stalled Democracy*, p. 168.
14 D. Azzellini and M. Kraft (eds), *The Class Strikes Back* (Boston, MA: Brill, 2018), p. 4. Available at Brill https://doi.org/10.1163/9789004291478 (accessed 20 November 2020).
15 Azzellini and Kraft (eds), *The Class Strikes Back*, pp. 9–15.
16 *Ibid.*, p. 11.
17 Wafa Noun (2020), interviewed by Lea Bou Khater, 25 March.

Appendices

	Federation (F.)	Date of creation
1	League of trade unions of workers and employees in Lebanon	1948
2	United F. of workers and employees in Lebanon	1952
3	F. of trade unions of workers in maritime transport	1954
4	F. of trade unions of workers and employees in North Lebanon	1954
5	F. of independent trade unions in Lebanon	1954
6	F. of trade unions of workers in independent authorities and public and private institutions	1963
7	National F. of trade unions of workers and employees in Lebanon	1966
8	F. of trade unions of workers and employees in South Lebanon	1966
9	F. of trade unions of workers in independent authorities and public institutions	1967
10	General F. of sectorial trade unions in Lebanon	1970
11	F. of trade unions of workers and employees in oil refining in Lebanon	1970
12	Technical F. of trade unions of workers and employees in chemical materials	1971
13	F. of trade unions of workers in printing and the media in Lebanon	1972
14	F. of trade unions of workers and employees in the trade sector	1972
15	F. of trade unions of workers and employees of airline companies	1972
16	F. of trade unions of workers and employees in the insurance sector in Lebanon	1973
17	F. of workers and employees in the health sector in Lebanon	1973
18	F. of trade unions of bank employees in Lebanon	1974

Appendix 1 (continued)

	Federation (F.)	Date of creation
19	F. of trade unions of workers and employees in food commodities	1976
20	F. of trade unions of workers and employees in the hotel and hospitality sector	1976
21	F. of trade unions of workers in construction and carpentry	1976
22	F. of trade unions of taxi drivers in land transport in Lebanon	1986
23	F. of trade unions of agricultural workers and peasants in Lebanon	1989
24	General F. of trade unions in the agricultural sector in Lebanon	1989
25	F. of trade unions of workers and employees in the Bekaa	1990
26	Lebanese F. of free trade unions	1991
27	Lebanese F. of trade unions of workers	1991
28	Lebanese F. of trade unions of taxi drivers and transport institutions	1994
29	F. of trade unions of agricultural workers in 'Amil	1994
30	F. of trade unions of workers and employees in metal, mechanics and plastics in South Lebanon	1994
31	F. of trade unions of workers and employees in Nabatiya	1994
32	F. of trade unions of workers and employees in the paper industry	1994
33	F. of national trade unions of workers in North Lebanon	1994
34	National F. of trade unions of workers and employees in South Lebanon	1994
35	F. of trade unions of workers in metal, mechanics and electronics	1995
36	F. of trade unions of workers and employees in Mount Lebanon	1996
37	National F. of Lebanese agricultural workers	1997
38	F. of trade unions of professional athletes in Lebanon	1997
39	F. of trade unions of workers in public services	1998
40	F. of trade unions of workers in modern technology	1998
41	F. of loyalty to trade unions of workers and employees in Lebanon	1998
42	F. of the renaissance of the workers in Lebanon	1998
43	F. of trade unions of workers in agriculture, tobacco and tombac in Lebanon	1999
44	F. of trade unions of agricultural workers in Lebanon	2003
45	F. of loyalty to trade unions of transport in Lebanon	2004
46	F. of trade unions of workers in cooperatives and vegetable markets in Lebanon	2004
47	F. of trade unions and employees in Baalbek-Hermel	2004

Appendix 1 (continued)

	Federation (F.)	Date of creation
48	F. of united trade unions of workers in Lebanon	2005
49	F. of trade unions of workers in Northern Mount Lebanon	2005
50	F. of trade unions of workers and employees in fuel oil	2005
51	F. of trade unions of workers and employees in Beirut	2005
52	Light F. of trade unions of workers and employees in Beirut and Mount Lebanon	2005
53	F. of vocational trade unions of workers in Lebanon	2005
54	F. of trade unions of workers in the health sector in Bekaa and Baalbek-Hermel	2005
55	F. of solidarity workers and employees in Lebanon	2005
56	F. of trade unions of local government workers and employees in Lebanon	2005
57	F. of trade unions of workers, employees and artisans in South Lebanon	2005
58	General F. of taxi drivers and transport workers in Lebanon	2014
59	F. of trade unions of workers in the gas and drilling sectors in Lebanon	2014

Appendix 2 Federations of trade unions by type, 2015

Date of creation	Type	Federation (F.)
1948	General	League of trade unions of workers and employees in Lebanon
1952	General	United F. of workers and employees in Lebanon
1954	General	F. of independent trade unions in Lebanon
1966	General	National F. for trade unions of workers and employees in Lebanon
1970	General	General F. of sectorial trade unions in Lebanon
1991	General	Lebanese F. of free trade unions
1991	General	Lebanese F. of trade unions of workers
1998	General	F. of loyalty to the trade unions of workers and employees in Lebanon
1998	General	F. of the renaissance of the workers in Lebanon
2005	General	F. of united trade unions of workers in Lebanon
2005	General	Light F. of trade unions of workers and employees in Beirut and Mount Lebanon
2005	General	F. of solidarity workers and employees in Lebanon
Total		12

Appendix 2 (continued)

Date of creation	Type	Federation (F.)
1954	Regional	F. of trade unions of workers and employees in North Lebanon
1966	Regional	F. of trade unions of workers and employees in South Lebanon
1986	Regional	F. of trade unions of taxi drivers in land transport in Lebanon
1990	Regional	F. of trade unions of workers and employees in the Bekaa
1994	Regional	F. of trade unions of workers and employees in Nabatiya
1994	Regional	F. of national trade unions of workers in North Lebanon
1994	Regional	National F. for trade unions of workers and employees in South Lebanon
1996	Regional	F. of trade unions of workers and employees in Mount Lebanon
2004	Regional	F. of trade unions and employees in Baalbek-Hermel
2005	Regional	F. of trade unions of workers in Northern Mount Lebanon
2005	Regional	F. of trade unions of workers and employees in Beirut
Total		11
1954	Sectorial	F. of trade unions of workers in maritime transport
1963	Sectorial	F. of trade unions of workers and employees in independent authorities and public and private institutions
1967	Sectorial	F. of trade unions of workers and employees in independent authorities and public institutions
1970	Sectorial	F. of trade unions of workers and employees in oil refining in Lebanon
1971	Sectorial	Technical F. of trade unions of workers and employees in chemical materials
1972	Sectorial	F. of trade unions of workers in printing and the media in Lebanon
1972	Sectorial	F. of trade unions of workers and employees in the trade sector
1972	Sectorial	F. of trade unions of workers and employees of airline companies
1973	Sectorial	F. of trade unions of the insurance sector in Lebanon
1973	Sectorial	F. of workers and employees in the health sector in Lebanon
1974	Sectorial	F. of trade unions of bank employees in Lebanon

Appendix 2 (continued)

Date of creation	Type	Federation (F.)
1976	Sectorial	F. of trade unions of workers and employees in food commodities
1976	Sectorial	F. of trade unions of workers and employees in the hotel and hospitality sector
1976	Sectorial	F. of trade unions of workers in construction and carpentry
1989	Sectorial	F. of trade unions of agricultural workers and peasants in Lebanon
1989	Sectorial	General F. of trade unions in the agricultural sector in Lebanon
1994	Sectorial	Lebanese F. of trade unions of taxi drivers and transport institutions
1994	Sectorial	F. of trade unions of agricultural workers in 'Amil
1994	Sectorial	F. of trade unions of workers and employees in the paper industry
1995	Sectorial	F. of trade unions of workers in metal, mechanics and electronics
1997	Sectorial	National F. of Lebanese agricultural workers
1997	Sectorial	F. of trade unions of professional athletes in Lebanon
1998	Sectorial	F. of trade unions of workers in public services
1998	Sectorial	F. of trade unions of workers in modern technology
1999	Sectorial	F. of trade unions of workers in agriculture, tobacco and tombac in Lebanon
2003	Sectorial	F. of trade unions of agricultural workers in Lebanon
2004	Sectorial	F. of loyalty to trade unions of transport in Lebanon
2004	Sectorial	F. of trade unions of workers cooperatives and vegetable markets in Lebanon
2005	Sectorial	F. of trade unions of workers and employees in fuel oil
2005	Sectorial	F. of vocational trade unions of workers in Lebanon
2005	Sectorial	F. of trade unions of workers and employees of municipalities in Lebanon
2014	Sectorial	General F. of taxi drivers and transport workers in Lebanon
2014	Sectorial	F. of trade unions of workers in the gas and drilling sector in Lebanon
Total		33
1994	Sectorial-Regional	F. of trade unions of workers and employees in metal, mechanics and plastics in South Lebanon
2005	Sectorial-Regional	F. of trade unions of workers in the health sector in Bekaa and Baalbek-Hermel

Appendix 2 (continued)

Date of creation	Type	Federation (F.)	
2005	Sectorial-Regional	F. of trade unions of employees, workers and artisans in South Lebanon	
Total			3
Overall total			59

Appendix 3 Federations of trade unions by date of last elections, 2015

Federation (F.)	Last elections
Lebanese F. of trade unions of taxi drivers and transport institutions	1994
National F. of Lebanese agricultural workers	1997
F. of trade unions of professional athletes in Lebanon	1997
F. of trade unions of agricultural workers and peasants in Lebanon	2005
F. of united trade unions of workers in Lebanon	2005
F. of trade unions of workers in Northern Mount Lebanon	2005
F. of trade unions of workers and employees in fuel oil	2005
F. of trade unions of workers in printing and the media in Lebanon	2007
F. of trade unions of agricultural workers in Jabal 'Amil	2007
F. of trade unions of workers and employees in metal, mechanics and plastics in South Lebanon	2007
F. of trade unions of workers in agriculture, tobacco and tombac in Lebanon	2007
F. of trade unions of workers and employees in food commodities	2009
League of trade unions of workers and employees in Lebanon	2010
F. of trade unions of workers in maritime transport	2010
National F. for trade unions of workers and employees in Lebanon	2010
General F. of sectorial trade unions in Lebanon	2010
F. of trade unions of workers and employees in the trade sector	2010
F. of trade unions of the insurance sector in Lebanon	2010
F. of trade unions of workers and employees in the Bekaa	2010
Lebanese F. of free trade unions	2010
Lebanese F. of trade unions of workers	2010
F. of trade unions of workers in public services	2010
F. of trade unions of workers in modern technology	2010
F. of trade unions of agricultural workers in Lebanon	2010
United F. of workers and employees in Lebanon	2011
F. of trade unions of workers and employees in North Lebanon	2011
F. of trade unions of workers in independent authorities and public institutions	2011
Technical F. of trade unions of workers and employees in chemical materials	2011

Appendix 3 (continued)

Federation (F.)	Last elections
F. of loyalty to trade unions of transport in Lebanon	2011
F. of independent trade unions in Lebanon	2013
F. of trade unions of workers and employees of airline companies	2013
F. of workers and employees in the health sector in Lebanon	2013
F. of trade unions of workers and employees in the hotel and hospitality sector	2013
F. of trade unions of workers and employees in Nabatiya	2013
F. of trade unions of workers in metal, mechanics and electronics	2013
F. of loyalty to trade unions of workers and employees in Lebanon	2013
F. of trade unions of workers in cooperatives and vegetable markets in Lebanon	2013
F. of trade unions of workers and employees in Beirut	2013
F. of trade unions of workers in independent authorities and public and private institutions	2014
F. of trade unions of workers and employees in South Lebanon	2014
F. of trade unions of taxi drivers in land transport in Lebanon	2014
F. of trade unions of workers and employees in the paper industry	2014
F. of trade unions and employees in Baalbek-Hermel	2014
Light F. of trade unions of workers and employees in Beirut and Mount Lebanon	2014
F. of vocational trade unions of workers in Lebanon	2014
F. of trade unions of workers in the health sector in Bekaa and Baalbek-Hermel	2014
General F. of taxi drivers and transport workers in Lebanon	2014
F. of trade unions of workers in the gas and drilling sectors in Lebanon	2014
F. of trade unions of workers and employees in oil refining in Lebanon	2015
F. of trade unions of bank employees in Lebanon	2015
F. of trade unions of workers in construction and carpentry	2015
General F. of trade unions in the agricultural sector in Lebanon	2015
F. of national trade unions of workers in North Lebanon	2015
National F. for trade unions of workers and employees in South Lebanon	2015
F. of the renaissance of the workers in Lebanon	2015
F. of solidarity workers and employees in Lebanon	2015
F. of trade unions of workers and employees of municipalities in Lebanon	2015
F. of trade unions of employees, workers and artisans in South Lebanon	2015
F. of trade unions of workers and employees in Mount Lebanon	N/A

Appendix 4 Federations and trade unions, 2015

No.	Federation (F.)	Trade unions (T.U.)	Date of creation (if known)	Total T.U. in F.
1	League of trade unions of workers and employees in Lebanon	Building and construction		4
		Workers in the trade sector in Lebanon		
		Employees and workers in grocery shops		
		Employees in cinema-film distribution		
2	United F. of workers and employees in Lebanon	Workers and employees of Lecico (ceramics manufacturer)	1960	5
		Car importers		
		Distributors of gas bottles		
		Workers and employees in automotive, mechanics and metal industries	1975	
		Workers and employees of the Lebanese Cement Company	1956	
3	F. of trade unions of workers in maritime transport	Sailors in the Port of Beirut		7
		Security guards in the Port of Beirut		
		Sailors and workers on vessels in the Port of Beirut	1948	
		Workers at seaports in Lebanon		
		Workers in fruit and vegetable transport in the Port of Beirut		
		Lebanese sailors in Lebanon	1972	
		Employees of travel and boat-charter agencies in Lebanon		
4	F. of trade unions of workers and employees in North Lebanon	Drivers in North Lebanon		14
		Printing and binding workers in North Lebanon		
		Hotel and hospitality workers in North Lebanon		
		Mechanics workers in North Lebanon		
		Carpenters in North Lebanon		
		Workers in shoe and leather manufacture in North Lebanon		

Appendix 4 (continued)

No.	Federation (F.)	Trade unions (T.U.)	Date of creation (if known)	Total T.U. in F.
		Knitwear workers in North Lebanon	1956	
		Tailors in North Lebanon		
		Workers in and managers of cinemas in North Lebanon		
		Workers and employees of social services associations		
		Bank employees in North Lebanon		
		Workers and employees of EDL-Qadisha	1956	
		Workers and employees of the Iraq Oil Company		
		Workers and employees of the Tripoli oil refinery	1960	
5	F. of independent trade unions in Lebanon	Printing and binding workers in Lebanon		4
		Sewing and tailoring workers in Lebanon		
		Workers and employees in packaging and refrigeration in Lebanon	1975	
		Workers and employees in car plants, mechanics and metals		
6	F. of trade unions of workers in independent authorities and public and private institutions	Local government workers in Beirut		6
		Workers and employees of the water companies of the Bekaa		
		Workers and employees of the water company of Beirut and Mount Lebanon		
		Workers and employees of the water company of North Lebanon		
		Workers and employees in grain silos	1973	
		Workers and employees in the Port of Beirut	1947	

No.	Federation (F.)	Trade unions (T.U.)	Date of creation (if known)	Total T.U. in F.
7	National F. of trade unions of workers and employees in Lebanon	Laundry workers in Beirut and Mount Lebanon	1995	16
		Lebanese chefs	1947	
		Drivers and owners of taxicabs in Beirut		
		Shoe and leather-goods workers in Lebanon	1955	
		Workers in tiles and chemical materials		
		Bakery workers in Beirut and Mount Lebanon	1966	
		Printing workers in Beirut and Mount Lebanon		
		Workers in mechanics	1947	
		Carpenters in Beirut and Mount Lebanon	1947	
		Upholsterers in Beirut and Mount Lebanon	1947	
		Workers in plastics and chemical factories in Lebanon	1971	
		Sewing and knitwear workers in Beirut and Mount Lebanon	1985	
		Mill workers and employees in Lebanon		
		Oil-company workers in Lebanon	1982	
		Workers and employees in the electrical sector in Lebanon	1991	
		Workers and employees in restaurants, coffee shops and hotels in Lebanon	1947	
8	F. of trade unions of workers and employees in South Lebanon	Taxi drivers in South Lebanon	1994	16
		Bakery workers in South Lebanon		
		Workers in sanitary, heating and cooling installations in South Lebanon		
		Painters and decorators in Saida		
		Bamboo workers in Saida		

Appendix 4 (continued)

No.	Federation (F.)	Trade unions (T.U.)	Date of creation (if known)	Total T.U. in F.
		Workers in coffee shops, restaurants and hotels in Saida	1960	
		Carpenters in Saida		
		Fishermen in Saida	1953	
		Tile and marble workers in Saida		
		Workers in soap and detergents in Saida		
		Dairy workers in Saida		
		Sewing and knitwear workers in Saida		
		Workers and employees in the trade sector in South Lebanon	1954	
		Workers and employees in the Port of Saida		
		Workers and employees in al-Zahrani refineries	1963	
		Workers and employees of oil utilities in al-Zahrani	1986	
9	F. of trade unions of workers in independent authorities and public institutions	Workers and employees of the Office Nationale des Eaux du Litani	1969	4
		Workers and employees of the Oadisha electricity company		
		Workers and employees of Électricité du Liban (EDL)	1962	
		Employees of the National Social Security Fund	1968	
10	General F. of sectorial trade unions in Lebanon	F. of trade unions of air transport	1996	11
		F. of trade unions of workers and employees of airline companies	1972	
		F. of trade unions of agricultural workers in Jabal 'Amil	1994	
		F of trade unions of workers and employees in Nabatiya	1994	
		F. of trade unions of workers and employees in metal, mechanics and plastics in South Lebanon	1994	

Appendix 4 (continued)

No.	Federation (F.)	Trade unions (T.U.)	Date of creation (if known)	Total T.U. in F.
		F. of trade unions of workers and employees in the paper industry	1994	
		F. of trade unions of workers in metal, mechanics and electronics	1971	
		F. of trade unions of workers in independent authorities and public and private institutions	1963	
		Lebanese F. of taxi drivers and transport institutions	1994	
		National F. of trade unions of employees in South Lebanon	1994	
		Trade unions of workers and employees in the tobacco and tombac industries	1947	
11	F. of trade unions of workers and employees in oil refining in Lebanon	Workers and employees at the Zahrani oil terminal	1963	8
		Workers and employees at the Tripoli oil terminal		
		Workers and employees at Zahrani oil installations	1986	
		Workers and employees of companies of Mobile Oil Lebanon, Inc.	1947	
		Workers and employees of TotalEnergies Liban	1957	
		Workers and employees of MEDCO Petroleum in Lebanon		
		Workers and employees of IPCO Industrial Plastics in Lebanon	1968	
		Workers and employees at the Tripoli oil refinery	1960	
12	Technical F. of trade unions of workers and employees in chemical materials	Paint workers in Mount Lebanon		7
		Workers in fuel-oil distribution in Lebanon		
		Workers and employees of plastics and chemical factories in Lebanon		
		Workers and employees of gas companies in Lebanon		

Appendix 4 (continued)

No.	Federation (F.)	Trade unions (T.U.)	Date of creation (if known)	Total T.U. in F.
		Workers and employees of the Sibline cement and concrete company		
		Workers in soap and detergents in Mount Lebanon		
		Workers and employees of United Oil		
13	F. of trade unions of workers in printing and the media in Lebanon	Sellers of newspapers and magazines in Lebanon	1973	6
		Employees of newspapers, magazines and news agencies	1965	
		Print workers in Beirut and Mount Lebanon	1947	
		Printing and binding workers in Lebanon	1948	
		Journalism graduates in Lebanon		
		Employees of advertising agencies in Lebanon	1970	
14	F. of trade unions of workers and employees in the trade sector	Workers and employees of grain importers	1966	5
		Agricultural workers and employees in Lebanon	1971	
		Workers and employees in the textile trade in Lebanon	1976	
		Workers and employees in the carpet trade	1973	
		Workers and employees in the car spare-parts trade	1971	
15	F. of trade unions of workers and employees of airline companies	Workers and employees of the Lebanese national airline	1996	4
		Workers and employees of trans-Mediterranean airlines	1979	
		Workers and employees of the Lebanese operating company of Beirut airport	1995	
		Workers and employees of Middle East Airlines	1972	

Appendix 4 (continued)

No.	Federation (F.)	Trade unions (T.U.)	Date of creation (if known)	Total T.U. in F.
16	F. of trade unions of workers in the insurance sector in Lebanon	Workers and employees in insurance and mutual funds in Lebanon	1973	3
		Workers and employees of insurance companies in Lebanon		
		Agents of life-insurance companies		
17	F. of workers and employees in the health sector in Lebanon	Workers in medical clinics in Beirut		4
		Workers and employees in social services hospitals		
		Workers and employees of the Hôtel-Dieu de France hospital		
		Workers and employees of the Islamic Elderly Rest House	1980	
18	F. of trade unions of bank workers and employees in Lebanon	Bank employees in the Bekaa	1974	3
		Bank employees in South Lebanon	1990	
		Bank employees in Lebanon	1947	
19	F. of trade unions of workers and employees in food commodities	Lebanese chefs	1947	14
		Bakery workers in South Lebanon		
		Bakery workers in the Bekaa	1985	
		Bakery workers in North Lebanon		
		Workers in hotels, restaurants and cafés in North Lebanon		
		Bamboo workers in Saida		
		Bakery workers in Beirut and Mount Lebanon	1972	
		Workers in hotels, restaurants and cafés in Saida		
		Dairy workers in Saida		
		Mill workers and employees in Lebanon		
		Workers and employees of agricultural companies in the Bekaa		
		Workers and employees in fruit and vegetable packaging in the Bekaa		

Appendix 4 (continued)

No.	Federation (F.)	Trade unions (T.U.)	Date of creation (if known)	Total T.U. in F.
		Workers and employees in restaurants, cafés and hotels in Lebanon	1946	
		Workers and employees in poultry farms in the Bekaa		
20	F. of trade unions of workers and employees in the hotel and hospitality sector	Workers and employees of the Casino of Lebanon and other establishments	1994	5
		Workers and employees in cafés and restaurants in the Bekaa	1993	
		Workers and employees of the Lebanese Golf Club		
		Workers and employees in hotels and restaurants in Mount Lebanon and Beirut	1994	
		Workers and employees in hotels, restaurants and leisure centres	1958	
21	F. of trade unions of workers in construction and carpentry	Tile workers in Zahle and the Bekaa	1956	8
		Construction workers in North Lebanon		
		Construction workers in Beirut and Mount Lebanon		
		Construction workers in Tyre		
		Carpenters in North Lebanon	1952	
		Carpenters in Beirut and Mount Lebanon	1946	
		Upholsterers in Beirut and Mount Lebanon	1946	
		Painters and decorators in Lebanon		
22	F. of trade unions of taxi drivers in land transport in Lebanon	Drivers and owners of taxicabs in Beirut		3
		Drivers and owners of taxicabs in Mount Lebanon	1954	
		Drivers in North Lebanon		

No.	Federation (F.)	Trade unions (T.U.)	Date of creation (if known)	Total T.U. in F.
23	F. of trade unions of agricultural workers and peasants in Lebanon	Flower and plant growers in Lebanon		3
		Apple and mountain fruit-tree growers in Lebanon		
		Olive-tree growers in South Lebanon		
24	General F. of trade unions in the agricultural sector in Lebanon	Vineyard owners in Lebanon		4
		Agricultural workers in the Bekaa		
		Farmers in North Lebanon	1993	
		Fruit-tree growers in North Lebanon		
25	F. of trade unions of workers and employees in the Bekaa	Bakery workers	1985	6
		Tile workers		
		Workers in fruit and vegetable packaging	1990	
		Bank employees		
		Workers and employees of agricultural companies		
		Workers and employees in poultry farms		
26	Lebanese F. of free trade unions	Workers in metal, glass and pottery		6
		Workers and employees of furniture companies		
		Workers and employees in the car spare-parts trade		
		Workers and employees in private schools in Lebanon		
		Workers and employees in agriculture in Lebanon		
		Workers and employees in advertising and the media		
27	Lebanese F. of trade unions of workers	Workers and employees of furniture companies		5
		Workers and employees in hairdressing in Beirut	1947	
		Workers and employees in private schools in Lebanon		

Appendix 4 (continued)

No.	Federation (F.)	Trade unions (T.U.)	Date of creation (if known)	Total T.U. in F.
		Workers and employees in packaging and refrigeration in Lebanon	1999	
28	Lebanese F. of trade unions of taxi drivers and transport institutions	General trade union of taxi drivers in Lebanon	1966	6
		Taxi drivers in the Bekaa		
		Taxi drivers in North Lebanon		
		Taxi drivers in Mount Lebanon	1993	
		Taxi drivers in Nabatiya	1994	
		Drivers and owners of taxicabs in the north of Metn	1953	
29	F. of trade unions of agricultural workers in Jabal 'Amil	Livestock workers in Nabatiya		3
		Fruit-tree growers in South Lebanon	1993	
		Flower and plant growers in South Lebanon	1993	
30	F. of trade unions of workers and employees in metal, mechanics and plastics in South Lebanon	Workers in car mechanics and electronics in South Lebanon	1994	4
		Workers and employees in plastics and tyres in South Lebanon	1994	
		Car-paint workers in South Lebanon	1994	
		Metalworkers	1994	
31	F. of trade unions of workers and employees in Nabatiya	Tailors in South Lebanon	1990	3
		Construction and carpentry workers in South Lebanon	1993	
		Workers in shoe and leather-goods manufacturing in South Lebanon	1996	
32	F. of trade unions of workers and employees in the paper industry	Workers in paper-bag making in Lebanon		3
		Workers in cardboard production in Lebanon	1994	
		Workers in paper production in Lebanon	1974	

Appendix 4 (continued)

No.	Federation (F.)	Trade unions (T.U.)	Date of creation (if known)	Total T.U. in F.
33	F. of national trade unions of workers in North Lebanon	Taxi drivers in North Lebanon		3
		Workers and employees of the Port of Tripoli	1993	
		Workers in hairdressing and beauty salons in North Lebanon	2002	
34	National F. of trade unions of workers and employees in South Lebanon	Agricultural workers in South Lebanon	1988	3
		Workers and employees in hospitals in South Lebanon	1990	
		Workers and employees in gas and energy companies in South Lebanon	1990	
35	F. of trade unions of workers in metal, mechanics and electronics	Workers in metals, mechanics and refrigeration	1994	5
		Workers in light metal industries	1994	
		Workers in electricity and electronics in Lebanon	1994	
		Agents of the car registration authority	1994	
		Taxi drivers in Nabatiya	1994	
36	F. of trade unions of workers and employees in Mount Lebanon	Hospital workers in Mount Lebanon		4
		Textile and clothing workers in Lebanon		
		Workers and employees in the oxygen industry in Lebanon	1964	
		Workers and employees of United Oil		
37	National F. of Lebanese agricultural workers	Farmers in North Lebanon	1993	4
		Poultry farmers in the Bekaa	1993	
		Workers in livestock in the Bekaa	1994	
		Beetroot farmers		
38	F. of trade unions of professional athletes in Lebanon	Martial arts professionals in Lebanon		3
		Boxing professionals in Lebanon		
		Diving and sea sports professionals		

Appendix 4 (continued)

No.	Federation (F.)	Trade unions (T.U.)	Date of creation (if known)	Total T.U. in F.
39	F. of trade unions of workers in public services	Workers and employees of gas companies in Lebanon	1968	4
		Workers and employees of grain importers and exporters in Lebanon		
		Workers and employees of the Hôtel-Dieu de France hospital		
		Workers and employees of the Lebanese cement company	1956	
40	F. of trade unions of workers in modern technology	Computer operators	1976	7
		Workers in metal, glass and pottery	1991	
		Workers and employees in the electrical appliances sector in Lebanon	1991	
		Workers and employees in agriculture in Lebanon	1971	
		Workers and employees of advertising and media companies in Lebanon	1970	
		Workers and employees of car companies, mechanics and metals	1975	
		Computer programmers in Lebanon	1994	
41	F. of loyalty to trade unions of workers and employees in Lebanon	Electrical technicians in Beirut and Mount Lebanon		6
		Construction workers in the Bekaa	1994	
		Fish farmers in the Bekaa	1995	
		Workers and employees of cooperatives in Beirut and Mount Lebanon	1994	
		Workers and employees of hospitals in the Bekaa	1994	
		Construction contractors in Lebanon		
42	F. of the renaissance of the workers in Lebanon	Workers in the trade sector in Lebanon		4
		Workers in the industrial sector in Lebanon		

Appendix 4 (continued)

No.	Federation (F.)	Trade unions (T.U.)	Date of creation (if known)	Total T.U. in F.
		Construction workers and employees in Lebanon		
		Retail workers in Lebanon		
43	F. of trade unions of workers in agriculture, tobacco and tombac in Lebanon	Tobacco and tombac farmers in the Bekaa	1994	3
		Tobacco and tombac farmers in South Lebanon	1993	
		Tobacco and tombac farmers in North Lebanon	1994	
44	F. of trade unions of agricultural workers in Lebanon	Owners of olive-oil pressing companies in South Lebanon		15
		Workers in livestock in Baalbek-Hermel		
		Potato workers in Hermel		
		Fishermen in South Lebanon		
		Fishermen on the southern coast		
		Fishermen in Ouzai and neighbouring ports		
		Fish farmers and workers in South Lebanon		
		Poultry farmers in Baalbek-Hermel		
		Beekeepers in South Lebanon		
		Beekeepers in Jbeil and Kisirwan		
		Fruit-tree growers in South Lebanon		
		Fruit-tree growers in the Mid-South		
		Greenhouse farmers in Lebanon		
		Grain and olive farmers in the Bekaa		
		Banana, citrus and exotic tree-growers in the South		
45	F. of loyalty to trade unions of transport in Lebanon	Public minibus drivers in Lebanon	2001	4
		School-bus drivers in South Lebanon	2004	
		Minibus drivers for schools and universities in Lebanon		
		Drivers and employees in land transport in Lebanon	2005	

Appendix 4 (continued)

No.	Federation (F.)	Trade unions (T.U.)	Date of creation (if known)	Total T.U. in F.
46	F. of trade unions of workers in cooperatives and vegetable markets in Lebanon	Workers in fruit and vegetable markets in the Bekaa		4
		Workers and employees in cooperatives in Beirut and Mount Lebanon	1994	
		Workers and employees of companies and factories in the Bekaa		
		Workers and employees in cooperatives in the Bekaa		
47	F. of trade unions and employees in Baalbek-Hermel	Hairdressers in the Bekaa	1993	9
		Metalworkers in the Bekaa	1993	
		Carpenters in the Bekaa	1993	
		Car mechanics in the Bekaa	1993	
		Tobacco and tombac growers in the Bekaa	1993	
		Workers and employees in retail shops in the Bekaa	1993	
		Workers and employees in coffee shops and restaurants in the Bekaa		
		Workers and employees in butchers' shops in the Bekaa	1993	
		Workers and employees of water companies of the Bekaa		
48	F. of united trade unions of workers in Lebanon	Workers in gas distribution in Lebanon		4
		Workers and employees of grain importers and exporters in Lebanon		
		Workers and employees in the car spare-parts trade	1971	
		Workers and employees of car importers in Lebanon	2002	
49	F. of trade unions of workers in Northern Mount Lebanon	Hairdressers in Lebanon		6
		Workers and employees in the electrical appliances sector in Mount Lebanon	2004	

Appendix 4 (continued)

No.	Federation (F.)	Trade unions (T.U.)	Date of creation (if known)	Total T.U. in F.
		Workers and employees in insurance and mutual funds in Lebanon		
		Workers and employees of importers of domestic electrical appliances	1996	
		Workers and employees of car importers in Lebanon	2002	
		Workers and employees of the Casino du Liban	1980	
50	F. of trade unions of workers and employees in fuel oil	Workers and employees of fuel-oil and derivatives companies		3
		Workers and employees of gas companies in Lebanon		
		Workers and employees of fuel-oil companies in Lebanon	1982	
51	F. of trade unions of workers and employees in Beirut	Workers in chemists and medical clinics in Lebanon	2005	6
		Sailors in the port of Beirut		
		Workers and employees of Media Projects International		
		Workers and employees of Islamic charity projects		
		Workers and employees of the Hôtel-Dieu de France hospital		
		Workers and employees of the Islamic Elderly Rest House	1980	
52	Light F. of trade unions of workers and employees in Beirut and Mount Lebanon	Fishermen in Ouzai and neighbouring ports	2004	4
		Workers in industrial enterprises in southern Mount Lebanon	2005	
		Workers and employees of Ghandour companies	1973	
		Workers and employees in grocery shops		
53	F. of vocational trade unions of workers in Lebanon	Taxi drivers in Mount Lebanon	1993	6
		Metalworkers in the Bekaa	1993	
		Workers and employees in cafés and restaurants in the Bekaa	1993	

Appendix 4 (continued)

No.	Federation (F.)	Trade unions (T.U.)	Date of creation (if known)	Total T.U. in F.
		Workers and employees in gas and energy in South Lebanon	1990	
		Workers and employees in retail shops in the Bekaa	1993	
		Workers and employees in public schools in Lebanon	2005	
54	F. of trade unions of workers in the health sector in Bekaa and Baalbek-Hermel	Construction workers in the Bekaa		5
		Workers in fruit and vegetable markets in the Bekaa		
		Workers and employees in hospitals in the Bekaa	1994	
		Workers and employees in companies and factories in the Bekaa	2001	
		Workers and employees in cooperatives in the Bekaa		
55	F. of solidarity workers and employees in Lebanon	Workers in health services in Lebanon		3
		Workers and employees of Media Projects International		
		Workers and employees of the Islamic Elderly Rest House	1980	
56	F. of trade unions of local government workers and employees in Lebanon	Workers and employees of the municipalities of Nabatiya	2003	6
		Workers in the municipality of Beirut	1972	
		Workers in the municipality of Hareit Hrayk		
		Workers in the municipality of Tripoli	1980	
		Workers and employees in the municipalities of Baalbek-Hermel	2004	
		Workers and employees in the municipality of Tyre	2001	

Appendix 4 (continued)

No.	Federation (F.)	Trade unions (T.U.)	Date of creation (if known)	Total T.U. in F.
57	F. of trade unions of workers, employees and artisans in South Lebanon	School-bus drivers in South Lebanon	2004	7
		Fishermen on the southern coast		
		Greenhouse farmers in South Lebanon	1994	
		Local government workers and employees in South Lebanon	2005	
		Beekeepers in South Lebanon		
		Fruit-tree growers in the Mid-South		
		Banana, citrus and exotic tree-growers in South Lebanon		
58	General F. of taxi drivers and transport workers in Lebanon	General trade union of taxi drivers in Lebanon	1966	3
		Workers and employees in the car spare-parts trade	1971	
		Workers and employees in car manufacturing, mechanics and metals	1975	
59	F. of trade unions of workers in the gas and drilling sector in Lebanon	Workers in gas distribution in Lebanon		3
		Workers and employees of the TotalEnergies Liban	1957	
		Workers and employees of oil companies in Lebanon		

Index

Lightning Source UK Ltd.
Milton Keynes UK
UKHW020744170123
415455UK00008B/538

9 781526 159434